Clarel by Herman Melville

Part IV – (of IV) Bethlehem

Herman Melville was born in New York City on August 1st, 1819, the third of eight children.

At the age of 7 Melville contracted scarlet fever which was to permanently diminish his eyesight. At this time Melville was described as being "very backwards in speech and somewhat slow in comprehension."

His father died when he was 12 leaving the family in very straitened times. Just 14 Melville took a job in a bank paying $150 a year that he obtained via his uncle, Peter Gansevoort, who was one of the directors of the New York State Bank.

After a failed stint as a surveyor he signed on to go to sea and travelled across the Atlantic to Liverpool and then on further voyages to the Pacific on adventures which would soon become the architecture of his novels. Whilst travelling he joined a mutiny, was jailed, fell in love with a South Pacific beauty and became known as a figure of opposition to the coercion of native Hawaiians to the Christian religion.

He drew from these experiences in his books Typee, Omoo, and White-Jacket. These were published as novels, the first initially in London in 1846.

By 1851 his masterpiece, Moby Dick, was ready to be published. It is perhaps, and certainly at the time, one of the most ambitious novels ever written. However, it never sold out its initial print run of 3,000 and Melville's earnings on this masterpiece were a mere $556.37.

In succeeding years his reputation waned and he found life increasingly difficult. His family was growing, now four children, and a stable income was essential.

With his finances in a disappointing state Melville took the advice of friends that a change in career was called for. For many others public lecturing had proved very rewarding. From late 1857 to 1860, Melville embarked upon three lecture tours, where he spoke mainly on Roman statuary and sightseeing in Rome.

In 1876 he was at last able to publish privately his 16,000 line epic poem Clarel. It was to no avail. The book had an initial printing of 350 copies, but sales failed miserably.

On December 31st, 1885 Melville was at last able to retire. His wife had inherited several small legacies and provide them with a reasonable income.

Herman Melville, novelist, poet, short story writer and essayist, died at his home on September 28rh 1891 from cardiovascular disease.

Index of Contents
Part IV - Bethlehem

Canto I - In Saddle
Canto II - The Ensign
Canto III - The Island
Canto IV - An Intruder
Canto V - Of the Stranger
Canto VI - Bethlehem
Canto VII - At Table
Canto VIII - The Pillow
Canto IX - The Shepherds' Dale
Canto X - A Monument
Canto XI - Disquiet
Canto XII - Of Pope and Turk
Canto XIII - The Church of the Star
Canto XIV - Soldier and Monk
Canto XV - Symphonies
Canto XVI - The Convent Roof
Canto XVII - A Transition
Canto XVIII - The Hillside
Canto XIX - A New-Comer
Canto XX - Derwent and Ungar
Canto XXI - Ungar and Rolfe
Canto XXII - Of Wickedness the Word
Canto XXIII - Derwent and Rolfe
Canto XXIV - Twilight
Canto XXV - The Invitation
Canto XXVI - The Prodigal
Canto XXVII - By Parapet
Canto XXVIII - David's Well
Canto XXIX - The Night Ride
Canto XXX - The Valley of Decision
Canto XXXI - Dirge
Canto XXXII - Passion Week
Canto XXXIII - Easter
Canto XXXIV - Via Crucis
Canto XXXV - Epilogue
Herman Melville – A Short Biography
Herman Melville – A Concise Bibliography

Canto I - In Saddle

Of old, if legend truth aver,
With hearts that did in aim concur,
Three mitered kings—Amerrian,
Apelius, and Damazon—
By miracle in Cassak met
(An Indian city, bards infer);

Thence, prompted by the vision yet
To find the new-born Lord nor err,
Westward their pious feet they set—
With gold and frankincense and myrrh.
Nor failed they, though by deserts vast
And voids and menaces they passed:
They failed not, for a light was given—
The light and pilotage of heaven:
A light, a lead, no longer won
By any, now, who seekers are:
Or fable is it? but if none,
Let man lament the foundered Star.

And Kedron's pilgrims: In review
The wilds receive those guests anew.

Yet ere, the MANGER now to win,
Their desert march they re-begin,
Belated leaving Saba's tower;
Reverted glance they grateful throw,
Nor slight the abbot's parting dower
Whose benedictions with them go.
Nor did the sinner of the isle
From friendly cheer refrain, though lax:
"Our Lady of the Vines beguile
Your travel and bedew your tracks!"
Blithe wishes, which slim mirth bestow
For, ah, with chill at heart they mind
Two now forever left behind.
But as men drop, replacements rule:
Though fleeting be each part assigned,
The eternal ranks of life keep full:
So here if but in small degree—
Recruits for fallen ones atone;
The Arnaut and pilgrim from the sea
The muster joining; also one
In military undress dun—
A stranger quite.
The Arnaut rode
For escort mere. His martial stud
A brother seemed—as strong as he,
As brave in trappings, and with blood
As proud, and equal gravity,
Reserving latent mettle. Good
To mark the rider in his seat—
Tall, shapely, powerful and complete;
A 'lean, too, in an easy way,
Like Pisa's Tower confirmed in place

Nor lacking in subordinate grace
Of lighter beauty. Truth to say,
This horseman seemed to waive command:
Abeyance of the bridle-hand.
But winning space more wide and clear
He showed in ostentation here
How but a pulse conveyed through rein
Could thrill and fire, or prompt detain.
On dappled steed, in kilt snow-white,
With burnished arms refracting light,
He orbits round the plodding train.
Djalea in quiet seat observes;
'Tis little from his poise he swerves;
Sedate he nods, as he should say:
"Rough road may tame this holiday
Of thine; but pleasant to look on:
Come, that's polite!" for on the wing,
Or in suspense of curveting
Chiron salutes the Emir's son.

Meantime, remiss, with dangling sword,
Upon a cloistral beast but sad,
A Saba friar's befitting pad
(His own steed, having sprained a cord,
Left now behind in convent ward)
The plain-clad soldier, heeding none
Though marked himself, in neutral tone
Maintained his place. His shoulders lithe
Were long-sloped and yet ample, too,
In keeping with each limb and thew:
Waist flexile as a willow withe;
Withal, a slouched reserve of strength,
As in the pard's luxurious length;
The cheek, high-boned, of copperish show
Enhanced by sun on land and seas;
Long hair, much like a Cherokee's,
Curving behind the ear in flow
And veiling part a saber-scar
Slant on the neck, a livid bar;
Nor might the felt hat hide from view
One temple pitted with strange blue
Of powder-burn. Of him you'd say—
A veteran, no more. But nay:
Brown eyes, what reveries they keep—
Sad woods they be, where wild things sleep.
Hereby, and by yet other sign,
To Rolfe, and Clarel part, and Vine,
The stranger stood revealed, confessed

A native of the fair South-West—
Their countryman, though of a zone
Varied in nature from their own:
A countryman—but how estranged!
Nor any word as yet exchanged
With them. But yester-evening's hour
Then first he came to Saba's tower,
And saw the Epirot aside
In conference, and word supplied
Touching detention of the troop
Destined to join him for the swoop
Over Jordan. But the pilgrims few
Knew not hereof, not yet they knew,
But deemed him one who took his way
Eccentric in an armed survey
Of Judah.
　　　On the pearl-gray ass
(From Siddim riderless, alas!)
Rode now the timoneer sedate,
Jogging beneath the Druze's lee,
As well he might, instructed late
What perils in lack of convoy be.
A frater-feeling of the sea
Influenced Rolfe, and made him take
Solace with him of salt romance,
Albeit Agath scarce did wake
To full requital—chill, perchance
Derived from years or diffidence;
Howe'er, in friendly way Rolfe plied
One-sided chat.
　　　As on they ride
And o'er the ridge begin to go,
A parting glance they turn; and lo!
The convent's twin towers disappear—
Engulfed like a brig's masts below
Submerging waters. Thence they steer
Upward anew, in lane of steeps—
Ravine hewn-out, as 'twere by sledges;
Inwalled, from ledges unto ledges,
And stepwise still, each rider creeps,
Until, at top, their eyes behold
Judaea in highlands far unrolled.
A horseman so, in easier play
Wheeling aloft (so travelers say)
Up the Moor's Tower, may outlook gain
From saddle over Seville's plain.
But here, 'twixt tent-lapped hills, they see,
Northward, a land immovably

Haggard and haggish, specked gray-green—
Pale tint of those frilled lichens lean,
Which on a prostrate pine ye view,
When fallen from the banks of grace
Down to the sand-pit's sterile place,
Blisters supplant the beads of dew.
Canker and palmer-worm both must
Famished have left those fields of rust:
The rain is powder—land of dust:
There few do tarry, none may live—
Save mad, possessed, or fugitive.
Exalted in accursed estate,
Like Naaman in his leprous plight
Haughty before Elisha's gate,
Show the blanched hills.

All now alight
Upon the Promethean ledge.
The Druze stands by the imminent edge
Peering, and rein in hand. With head
Over her master's shoulder laid,
The mare, too, gazed, nor feared a check,
Though leaning half her lovesome neck,
Yet lightly, as a swan might do.
An arm Djalea enfolding stretched,
While sighs the sensitive creature fetched,
As e'en that waste to sorrow moved
Instinctive. So, to take the view
See man and mare, lover and loved.

Slant palm to brow against the haze,
Meantime the salt one sent his gaze
As from the mast-head o'er the pale
Expanse. But what may eyes avail?
Land lone as seas without a sail.
"Wreck, ho—the wreck!" Not unamazed
They hear his sudden outery. Crazed?
Or subject yet by starts dismayed
To flighty turns, for friars said
Much wandered he in mind when low.
But never Agath heeded them:
Forth did his leveled finger go
And, fixing, pointed: "See ye, see?
'Way over where the gray hills be;
Yonder—no, there that upland dim:
Wreck, ho! the wreck—Jerusalem!"
"Keen-sighted art thou!" said Djalea
Confirming him; "ay, it is there."

Then Agath, that excitement gone,
Relapsed into his quiet tone.

Canto II - The Ensign

Needs well to know the distant site
(Like Agath, who late on the way
From Joppa here had made delay)
Ere, if unprompted, thou aright
Mayst single Zion's mountain out
From kindred summits roundabout.
Abandoned quarry mid the hills
Remote, as well one's dream fulfills
Of what Jerusalem should be,
As that vague heap, whose neutral tones
Blend in with Nature's, helplessly:
Stony metropolis of stones.
But much as distant shows the town
Erst glorious under Solomon,
Appears now, in these latter days,
To languid eyes, through dwelling haze,
The city St. John saw so bright
With sardonyx and ruby? Gleam
No more, like Monte Rosa's hight,
Thy towers, O New Jerusalem?
To Patmos now may visions steal?
Lone crag where lone the ospreys wheel!

Such thought, or something near akin,
Touched Clarel, and perchance might win
(To judge them by their absent air)
Others at hand. But not of these
The Illyrian bold: impatient stare
He random flung; then, like a breeze
Which fitful rushes through the glen
Over clansmen low—Prince Charlie's men—
Shot down the ledges, while the clang
Of saber 'gainst the stirrup rang,
And clinked the steel shoe on the stone.
His freak of gallantry in cheer
Of barbarous escort ending here,
Back for the stronghold dashed he lone.
When died the din, it left them more
Becalmed upon that hollow shore.

Not slack was ocean's wrinkled son

In study of the mountain town—
Much like himself, indeed, so gray
Left in life's waste to slow decay.
For index now as he stretched forth
His loose-sleeved arm in sailor way
Pointing the bearings south and north,
Derwent, arrested, cried, "Dost bleed?"
Touching the naked skin: "Look here
A living fresco!" And indeed,
Upon the fore-arm did appear
A thing of art, vermil and blue,
A crucifixion in tattoo,
With trickling blood-drops strange to see.

Above that emblem of the loss,
Twin curving palm-boughs draping met
In manner of a canopy
Over an equi-limbed small cross
And three tri-spiked and sister crowns:
And under these a star was set:
And all was tanned and toned in browns.
In chapel erst which knew the mass,
A mullioned window's umber glass
Dyed with some saintly legend old,
Obscured by cobwebs; this might hold
Some likeness to the picture rare
On arm here webbed with straggling hair.
"Leave out the crucifixion's hint,"
Said Rolfe, "the rest will show in tint
The Ensign: palms, cross, diadems,
And star—the Sign!—Jerusalem's,
Coeval with King Baldwin's sway.—
Skilled monk in sooth ye need have sought
In Saba."
Quoth the sea-sage: "Nay;
Sketched out it was one Christmas day
Off Java-Head. Little I thought
(A heedless lad, scarce through youth's straits—
How hopeful on the wreckful way)
What meant this thing which here ye see,
The bleeding man upon the tree;
Since then I've felt it, and the fates."
"Ah—yes," sighed Derwent; "yes, indeed!
But 'tis the Ensign now we heed."
The stranger here his dusk eye ran
In reading sort from man to man,
Cleric to sailor—back again.
"But, shipmate," Derwent cried; "tell me:

How came you by this blazonry?"
"We seamen, when there's naught to do
In calms, the straw for hats we plait,
Or one another we tattoo
With marks we copy from a mate,
Which he has from his elders ta'en,
And those from prior ones again;
And few, if any, think or reck
But so with pains their skin to deck.
This crucifixion, though, by some
A charm is held 'gainst watery doom."

"Comrades," said Rolfe, "'tis here we note
Downhanded in a way blind-fold,
A pious use of times remote.
Ah, but it dim grows, and more dim,
The gold of legend, that fine gold!
Washed in with wine of Bethlehem,
This Ensign in the ages old
Was stamped on every pilgrim's arm
By grave practitioners elect
Whose calling lacked not for respect
In Zion. Like the sprig of palm,
Token it was at home, that he
Which bore, had kneeled at Calvary.
Nay, those monk-soldiers helmet-crowned,
Whose effigies in armed sleep, lie—
Stone, in the stony Temple round
In London; and (to verify
Them more) with carved greaves crossed, for sign
Of duty done in Palestine;
Exceeds it, pray, conjecture fair,
These may have borne this blazon rare,
And not alone on standard fine,
But pricked on chest or sinewy arm,
Pledged to defend against alarm
His tomb for whom they warred? But see,
From these mailed Templars now the sign,
Losing the import and true key,
Descends to boatswains of the brine."

Clarel, reposing there aside,
By secret thought preoccupied,
Now. as he inward chafe would shun,
A feigned quick interest put on:
"The import of these marks? Tell me."
"Come, come," cried Derwent; "dull ye bide!
By palm-leaves here are signified

Judaea, as on the Roman gem;
The cross scarce needs a word, agree;
The crowns are for the magi three;
This star—the star of Bethlehem."
"One might have known;" and fell anew
In void relapse.
"Why, why so blue?"
Derwent again; and rallying ran:
"While now for Bethlehem we aim,
Our stellar friend the post should claim
Of guide. We'll put him in the van—
Follow the star on the tattooed man,
We wise men here.—What's that?"
A gun,
At distance fired, startles the group.
Around they gaze, and down and up;
But in the wilds they seem alone.
Long time the echo sent its din,
Hurled roundabout, and out and in—
A foot-ball tossed from crag to crag;
Then died away in ether thin—
Died, as they deemed, yet did but lag,
For all abrupt one far rebound
Gave pause; that o'er, the hush was crowned.
"We loiter," Derwent said, in tone
Uneasy; "come, shall we go on?"
"Wherefore?" the saturnine demands.
Toward him they look, for his eclipse
There gave way for the first; and stands
The adage old, that one's own lips
Proclaim the character: "A gun:
A gun's man's voice—sincerest one.
Blench we to have assurance here,
Here in the waste, that kind is near?"
Eyes settle on his scars in view,
Both warp and burn, the which evince
Experience of the thing he hints.
"Nay—hark!" and all turn round anew:
Remoter shot came duller there:
"The Arnaut—and but fires in air,"
Djalea averred: "his last adieu."

By chance directed here in thought,
Clarel upon that warrior haught
Low mused: The rowel of thy spur
The robe rips of philosopher!
Naught reckest thou of wisest book:
The creeds thou star'st down with a look.

And how the worse for such wild sense?
And where is wisdom's recompense?
And as for heaven—Oh, heavens enlarge
Beyond each designated marge:
Valhalla's hall would hardly bar
Welcome to one whose end need be
In grace and grief of harnessed war,
To sink mid swords and minstrelsy.

So willful! but 'tis loss and smart,
Clarel, in thy dissolving heart.
Will't form anew?
Vine's watchful eye,
While none perceived where bent his view,
Had fed on Agath sitting by;
He seemed to like him, one whose print
The impress bore of Nature's mint
Authentic; man of nature true,
If simple; naught that slid between
Him and the elemental scene—
Unless it were that thing indeed
Uplooming from his ancient creed;
Yet that but deepen might the sense
Of awe, and serve dumb reverence
And resignation.—"Anywhere,"
Asked Vine here now to converse led—
"In those far regions, strange or rare,
Where thou hast been, may aught compare
With Judah here?"
"Sooth, sir," he said,
"Some chance comparison I've made
In mind, between this stricken land
And one far isle forever banned
I camped on in life's early days:
I view it now—but through a haze:
Our boats I view, reversed, turned down
For shelter by the midnight sea;
The very slag comes back to me
I raked for shells, but found not one;
That harpy sea-hawk—him I view
Which, pouncing, from the red coal drew
Our hissing meat—we lounging nigh—
An instant's dash—and with it flew
To his sea-rock detached, his cry
Thence sent, to mock the marl we threw:—
I hear, I see; return those days
Again—but 'tis through deepening haze:
How like a flash that life is gone—

So brief the youth by sailors known!"

"But tell us, tell," now others cried
And grouped them as by hearth-stone wide.
The timoneer, at hazard thrown
With men of order not his own,
Evinced abashment, yes, proved shy.
They urged; and he could but comply.
But, more of clearness to confer—
Less dimly to express the thing
Rude outlined by this mariner,
License is claimed in rendering;
And tones he felt but scarce might give,
The verse essays to interweave.

Canto III - The Island

"In waters where no charts avail,
Where only fin and spout ye see,
The lonely spout of hermit-whale,
God set that isle which haunteth me.
There clouds hang low, but yield no rain—
Forever hang, since wind is none
Or light; nor ship-boy's eye may gain
The smoke-wrapped peak, the inland one
Volcanic; this, within its shroud
Streaked black and red, burns unrevealed;
It burns by night—by day the cloud
Shows leaden all, and dull and sealed.
The beach is cinders. With the tide
Salt creek and ashy inlet bring
More loneness from the outer ring
Of ocean."
Pause he made, and sighed.—
"But take the way across the marl,
A broken field of tumbled slabs
Like ice-cakes frozen in a snarl
After the break-up in a sound;
So win the thicket's upper ground
Where silence like a poniard stabs,
Since there the low throb of the sea
Not heard is, and the sea-fowl flee
Far offthe shore, all the long day
Hunting the flying-fish their prey.

Haply in bush ye find a path:

Of man or beast it scarce may be;
And yet a wasted look it hath,
As it were traveled ceaselessly—
Century after century—
The rock in places much worn down
Like to some old, old kneeling-stone
Before a shrine. But naught's to see,
At least naught there was seen by me,
Of any moving, creeping one.

No berry do those thickets bear,
Nor many leaves. Yet even there,
Some sailor from the steerage den
Put sick ashorc alas, by men
Who, weary of him, thus abjure—
The way may follow, in pursuit
Of apples red—the homestead-fruit
He dreams of in his calenture.
He drops, lost soul; but we go on—
Advance, until in end be won
The terraced orchard's mysteries,
Which well do that imp-isle beseem;
Paved with jet blocks those terraces,
The surface rubbed to unctuous gleam
By something which has life, you feel:
And yet, the shades but death reveal;
For under cobwebbed cactus trees,
White by their trunks—what hulks be these
Which, like old skulls of Anaks, are
Set round as in a Golgotha?
But, list,—a sound! Dull, dull it booms—
Dull as the jar in vaulted tombs
When urns are shifted. With amaze
Into the dim retreats ye gaze.
Lo, 'tis the monstrous tortoise drear!
Of huge humped arch, the ancient shell
Is trenched with seams where lichens dwell,
Or some adhesive growth and sere:
A lumpish languor marks the pace
A hideous, harmless look, with trace
Of hopelessness; the eyes are dull
As in the bog the dead black pool:
Penal his aspect; all is dragged,
As he for more than years had lagged—
A convict doomed to bide the place;
A soul transformed—for earned disgrace
Degraded, and from higher race.
Ye watch him—him so woe-begone:

Searching, he creeps with laboring neck,
Each crevice tries, and long may seek:
Water he craves, where rain is none
Water within the parching zone,
Where only dews of midnight fall
And dribbling lodge in chinks of stone.
For meat the bitter tree is all—
The cactus, whose nipped fruit is shed
On those bleached skull-like hulks below,
Which, when by life inhabited,
Crept hither in last journey slow
After a hundred years of pain
And pilgrimage here to and fro,
For other hundred years to reign
In hollow of white armor so—
Then perish piecemeal. You advance:
Instant, more rapid than a glance,
Long neck and four legs are drawn in,
Letting the shell down with report
Upon the stone; so falls in court
The clattering buckler with a din.
There leave him, since for hours he'll keep
That feint of death.—But for the isle
Much seems it like this barren steep:
As here, few there would think to smile."

So, paraphrased in lines sincere
Which still similitude would win,
The sketch ran of that timoneer.
He ended, and how passive sate:
Nature's own look, which might recall
Dumb patience of mere animal,
Which better may abide life's fate
Than comprehend.
What may man know?
(Here pondered Clarel;) let him rule—
Pull down, build up, creed, system, school,
And reason's endless battle wage,
Make and remake his verbiage—
But solve the world! Scarce that he'll do:
Too wild it is, too wonderful.
Since this world, then, can baffle so—
Our natural harbor—it were strange
If that alleged, which is afar,
Should not confound us when we range
In revery where its problems are.—
Such thoughts! and can they e'en be mine
In fount? Did Derwent true divine

Upon the tower of Saba—yes,
Hinting I too much felt the stress
Of Rolfe—or whom? Green and unsure,
And in attendance on a mind
Poised at self-center and mature,
Do I but lacquey it behind?
Yea, here in frame of thought and word
But wear the cast clothes of my lord?

Canto IV - An Intruder

Quiet Agath, with a start, just then
Shrieked out, abhorrent or in fright.
Disturbed in its pernicious den
Amid dry flints and shards of blight,
A crabbed scorpion, dingy brown,
With nervous tail slant upward thrown
(Like to a snake's wroth neck and head
Dilating when the coil's unmade
Before the poor affrighted clown
Whose foot offends it unbeknown)
Writhing, faint crackling, like wire spring,
With anguish of the poisonous bile
Inflaming the slim duct, the while
In act of shooting toward the sting;
This, the unblest, small, evil thing,
'Tis this they mark, wriggling in range,
Fearless, and with ill menace, strange
In such a minim.

Derwent rose,
And Clarel; Vine and Rolfe remained
At gaze; the soldier too and Druze.
Cried Rolfe, while thus they stood enchained:
"O small epitome of devil,
Wert thou an ox couldst thou thus sway?
No, disproportionate is evil
In influence. Evil do I say?
But speak not evil of the evil:
Evil and good they braided play
Into one cord."
While they delay,
The object vanished. Turning head
Toward the salt one, Derwent said:
"The thing's not sweet; but why start so,
My good man, you that frequent know

The wonders of the deep?" He flushed,
And in embarrassment kept dumb.
But Rolfe here to the rescue pushed:
"Men not deemed craven will succumb
To such an apparition. Why,
Soldiers, that into battle marching
Elastic pace with instep arching—
Sailors (and he's a sailor nigh)
Who out upon the jib-boom hie,
At world's end, in the midnight gale,
And wrestle with the thrashing sail,
The while the speared spar like a javelin flies
Slant up from thundering seas to skies
Electric:—these—I've known one start
Seeing a spider run athwart!"

In common-place here lightly blew
Across them through the desert air
A whiff from pipe that Belex smoked:
The Druze his sleek mare smooth bestroked,
Then gave a sign. One parting view
At Zion blurred, and on they fare.

Canto V - Of the Stranger

While Agath was his story telling
(Ere yet the ill thing worked surprise)
The officer with forest eyes
Still kept them dwelling, somber dwelling
On that mild merman gray. His mien
In part was that of one who tries
Something outside his own routine
Of memories, all too profuse
In personal pain monotonous.
And yet derived he little here,
As seemed, to soothe his mind—austere
With deep impressions uneffaced.
At chance allusion—at the hint
That the dragged tortoise bore the print
Of something mystic and debased,
How glowed the comment in his eyes:
No cynic fire sarcastic; nay,
But deeper in the startled sway
Of illustrations to surmise.
Ever on him they turned the look,
While yet the hearing not forsook

The salt seer while narration ran.
The desert march resumed, in thought
They dwell, till Rolfe the Druze besought
If he before had met this man—
So distant, though a countryman
By birth. Why, yes—had met him: see,
Drilling some tawny infantry
In shadow of a Memphian wall,
White-robed young conscripts up the Nile;
And, afterward, on Jaffa beach,
With Turkish captains holding speech
Over some cannon in a pile
Late landed—with the conic ball.
No more? No more the Druze let fall,
If more he knew.
Thought Rolfe: Ay me,
Ay me, poor Freedom, can it be
A countryman's a refugee?
What maketh him abroad to roam,
Sharing with infidels a home?
Is it the immense charred solitudes
Once farms? and chimney-stacks that reign
War-burnt upon the houseless plain
Of hearthstones without neighborhoods?
Is it the wilds whose memories own
More specters than the woods bestrown
With Varus' legions mossy grown?
Is't misrule after strife? and dust
From victor heels? Is it disgust
For times when honor's out of date
And serveth but to alienate?
The usurping altar doth he scout—
The Parsee of a sun gone out?
And this, may all this mar his state?
His very virtues, in the blench
And violence of fortune's wrench,
Alas, serve but to vitiate?
Strong natures have a strong recoil
Whose shock may wreck them or despoil.
Oh, but it yields a thought that smarts,
To note this man. Our New World bold
Had fain improved upon the Old;
But the hemispheres are counterparts.
So inly Rolfe; and did incline
In briefer question there to Vine,
Who could but answer him with eyes
Opulent in withheld replies.
And here without a thought to chide-

Feeling the tremor of the ground—
Reluctant touching on the wound
Unhealed yet in our mother's side;
Behooveth it to hint in brief
The rankling thing in Ungar's grief;
For bravest grieve.—That evil day,
Black in the New World's calendar—
The dolorous winter ere the war;
True Bridge of Sighs—so yet 'twill be
Esteemed in riper history—
Sad arch between contrasted eras;
The span of fate; that evil day
When the cadets from rival zones,
Tradition's generous adherers,
Their country's pick and flower of sons,
Abrupt were called upon to act—
For life or death, nor brook delay—
Touching construction of a pact,
A paper pact, with points abstruse
As theologic ones—profuse
In matter for an honest doubt;
And which, in end, a stubborn knot
Some cut but with the sword; that day
With its decision, yet could sway
Ungar, and plunging thoughts excite.
Reading and revery imped his pain,
Confirmed, and made it take a flight
Beyond experience and the reign
Of self; till, in a sort, the man
Grew much like that Pamphylian
Who, dying (as the fable goes)
In walks of Hades met with those
Which, though he was a sage of worth,
Did such new pregnancies implant,
Hadean lore, he did recant
All science he had brought from earth.
Herewith in Ungar, though, ensued
A bias, bitterness—a strain
Much like an Indian's hopeless feud
Under the white's aggressive reign.
Indian's the word; nor it impeach
For over-pointedness of speech;
No, let the story rearward run
And its propriety be shown:
Up Chesapeake in days of old,
By winding banks whose curves unfold
Cape after cape in bright remove,
Steered the ship Ark with her attendant Dove.

From the non-conformists' zeal or bile
Which urged, inflamed the civil check
Upon the dreaded Popish guile,
The New World's fairer flowers and dews
Welcomed the English Catholic:
Like sheltering arms the shores expand
To embrace and take to heart the crews.
Care-worn, sea-worn, and tempest-tanned,
Devout they hail that harbor green;
And, mindful of heaven's gracious Queen
And Britain's princess, name it Mary-Land.
It was from one of Calvert's friends
The exile of the verse descends;
And gifts, brave gifts, and martial fame
Won under Tilly's great command
That sire of after-sires might claim.
But heedless, in the Indian glade
He wedded with a wigwam maid,
Transmitting through his line, far down,
Along with touch in lineaments,
A latent nature, which events
Developed in this distant son,
And overrode the genial part—
An Anglo brain, but Indian heart.
And yet not so but Ungar knew
(In freak, his forest name alone
Retained he now) that instinct true
Which tempered him in years bygone,
When, spite the prejudice of kin
And custom, he with friends could be
Outspoken in his heart's belief
That holding slaves was aye a grief—
The system an iniquity
In those who plant it and begin;
While for inheritors—alas
Who knows? and let the problem pass.
But now all that was over—gone;
Now was he the self-exiled one.
Too steadfast! Wherefore should be lent
The profitless high sentiment?

Renounce conviction in defeat:
Pass over, share the spoiler's seat
And thrive. Behooves thee else turn cheek
To fate with wisdom of the meek.
Wilt not? Unblest then with the store
Of heaven, and spurning worldly lore
Astute, eat thou thy cake of pride,

And henceforth live on unallied.—
His passion, that—mused, never said;
And his own pride did him upbraid.

The habit of his mind, and tone
Tenacious touching issues gone,
Expression found, nor all amiss,
In thing he'd murmur: it was this:
"Who abideth by the dead
Which ye hung before your Lord?
Steadfast who, when all have fled
Tree and corse abhorred?
Who drives off the wolf, the kite—
Bird by day, and beast by night,
And keeps the hill through all?
It is Rizpah: true is one
Unto death; nor then will shun
The Seven throttled and undone,
To glut the foes of Saul."

That for the past; and for the surge
Reactionary, which years urge:
"Elating and elate,
Do they mount them in their pride?
Let them wait a little, wait,
For the brimming of the flood
Brings the turning of the tide."

His lyric. Yet in heart of hearts
Perchance its vanity he knew,
At least suspected. What to do?
Time cares not to avenge your smarts,
But presses on, impatient of review.

Canto VI - Bethlehem

Over uplands now toward eve they pass
By higher uplands tinged with grass.
Lower it crept as they went on—
Grew in advance, and rugged the ground;
Yea, seemed before these pilgrims thrown
To carpet them to royal bound.
Each rider here in saddle-seat
Lounges relaxed, and glads his sight;
Solomon whinnies; those small feet
Of Zar tread lightly and more light:

Even Agath's ass the awakened head
Turns for a nibble. So they sped,
Till now Djalea turns short aside,
Ascends, and by a happy brink
Makes halt, and beckons them to ride
And there with him at pleasure drink
A prospect good.
Below, serene
In olive yards and vineyards fair,

They view a theater pale green
Of terraces, which stair by stair
Rise toward most venerable walls
On summits twin, and one squared heap
Of buttressed masonry based deep
Adown the crag on lasting pedestals.
Though on that mount but towers convene,
And hamlet none nor cot they see,
They cannot choose but know the scene;
And Derwent's eyes show humidly:
"What other hill? We view it here:
Blessed in story, and heart-cheer,
Hail to thee, Bethlehem of Judaea!

Oh, look: as if with conscious sense
Here nature shows meet reverence:
See, at the sacred mountain's feet
How kneels she with her fragrance sweet,
And swathes them with her grasses fair:
So Mary with the spikenard shed
A lowly love, and bowed her head
And made a napkin of her trailing hair."

He turned, but met no answering eyes;
The animation of surprise
Had vanished; strange, but they were dumb:
What wayward afterthought had come?
Those dim recurrings in the mind,
Sad visitations ill defined,
Which led the trio erst that met
Upon the crown of Olivet
Nehemiah's proffer to decline
When he invited them away
To Bethany—might such things sway
Even these by Bethlehem? The sign
Derwent respected, and he said
No more. And so, with spirits shrunk
Over the placid hills they tread

And win the stronghold of the monk.

Canto VII - At Table

As shipwrecked men adrift, whose boat
In war-time on the houseless seas
Draws nigh to some embattled hull
With pinnacles and traceries—
Grim abbey on the wave afloat;
And mark her bulwarks sorrowful
With briny stains, and answering mien
And cenobite dumb discipline,
And homely uniform of crew
Peering from ports where cannon lean,
Or pacing in deep galleries far,
Black cloisters of the god of war;
And hear a language which is new
Or foreign: so now with this band
Who, after desert rovings, win
The fort monastic, close at hand,
Survey it, meditate it—see,
Through vaultings, the girt Capuchin,
Or list his speech of Italy.

Up to the arch the graybeard train
Of Bethlehemites attend, salute,
And in expectancy remain
At stand; their escort ending here,
They wait the recompense and fruit;
'Tis given; and with friendly cheer
Parting, they bear a meed beyond
The dry price set down in the bond.
The bonus Derwent did suggest,
Saying: "They're old: of all sweet food
Naught they take in so cheers their blood
As ruddy coin; it pads the vest."
Belex abides—true as his steel
To noble pilgrims which such largess deal.
While these now at refection sit,
Rolfe speaks: "Provided for so well,
Much at our ease methinks we dwell.
Our merit's guerdon? far from it!
Unworthy, here we welcome win
Where Mary found no room at inn."
"True, true," the priest sighed, staying there
The cup of Bethlehem wine in hand;

Then sipped; yet by sad absent air
The flavor seeming to forswear;
Nor less the juice did glad the gland.
The abstemious Ungar noted all,
Grave silence keeping. Rolfe let fall:
"Strange! of the sacred places here,
And all through Palestine indeed,
Not one we Protestants hold dear
Enough to tend and care for."
"Pray, "
The priest, "and why now should that breed
Astonishment? but say your say."
"Why, Shakespeare's house in Stratford town
Ye keep with loving tendance true,
Set it apart in reverence due:
A shrine to which the pilgrim's won
Across an ocean's stormy tide:
What zeal, what faith is there implied;
Pure worship localized in grace,
Tradition sole providing base."
"Your drift I catch. And yet I think
That they who most and deepest drink
At Shakespeare's fountain, scarce incline
To idolize the local shrine:
What's in mere place that can bestead?"
"Nay, 'tis the heart here, not the head.
You note some pilgrims hither bring
The rich or humble offering:
If that's irrational—what then?
In kindred way your Lutheran
Will rival it; yes, in sad hour
The Lutheran widow lays her flower
Before the picture of the dead:
Vital affections do not draw
Precepts from Reason's arid law."
"Ah, clever! But we won't contend.
As for these Places, my dear friend,
Thus stands the matter—as you know:
Ere Luther yet made his demur,
These legend-precincts high and low
In custody already were
Of Greek and Latin, who retain.
So, even did we wish to be
Shrine-keepers here and share the fee—
No sites for Protestants remain."

The compline service they attend;
Then bedward, travel-worn, they wend;

And, like a bland breeze out of heaven,
The gracious boon of sleep is given.

But Ungar, islanded in thought
Which not from place a prompting caught,
Alone, upon the terrace stair
Lingered, in adoration there
Of Eastern skies: "Now night enthrones
Arcturus and his shining sons;
And lo, Job's chambers of the South:
How might his hand not go to mouth
In kiss adoring ye, bright zones?
Look up: the age, the age forget—
There's something to look up to yet!"

Canto VIII - The Pillow

When rule and era passed away
With old Sylvanus (stories say),
The oracles adrift were hurled,
And ocean moaned about the world,
And wandering voices without name
At sea to sailors did proclaim,
Pan, Pan is dead!
Such fables old—
From man's deep nature are they rolled,
Pained and perplexed—awed, overawed
By sense of change? But never word
Aerial by mortal heard,
Rumors that vast eclipse, if slow,
Whose passage yet we undergo,
Emerging on an age untried.

If not all oracles be dead,
The upstart ones the old deride:
Parrots replace the sibyls fled—
By rote repeat in lilting pride:

Lodged in power, enlarged in all,
Man achieves his last exemption—
Hopes no heaven, but fears no fall,
King in time, nor needs redemption.

They hymn. But these who cloistral dwell
In Bethlehem here, and share faith's spell
Meekly, and keep her tenor mild—

What know they of a world beguiled?
Or, knowing, they but know too well.

Buzzed thoughts! To Rolfe they came in doze
(His brain like ocean's murmuring shell)
Between the dream and slumber's light repose.

Canto IX - The Shepherds' Dale

"Up, up! Around morn's standard rally
She makes a sortie join the sally:
Up, slugabeds; up, up!"
That call
Ere matins did each pilgrim hear
In cell, and knew the blithe voice clear.
"Beshrew thee, thou'rt poetical,"
Rolfe murmured from his place withdrawn.
"Ay, brother; but 'tis not surprising:
Apollo's the god of early rising.
Up, up! The negro-groom of Night
Leads forth the horses of the Dawn!
Up, up!" So Derwent, jocund sprite—
Although but two days now were passed
Since he had viewed a sunrise last—
Persuaded them to join him there
And unto convent roof repair.
Thought one: He's of no nature surly,
So cheerful in the morning early.
Sun-worship over, they came down:
And Derwent lured them forth, and on.
Behind the Convent lies a dale,
The Valley of the Shepherds named,
(And never may the title fail!)
By old tradition fondly claimed
To be in truth the very ground
About whose hollow, on the mound
Of hills, reclined in dozing way
That simple group ere break of day,
Which, startled by their flocks' dismay—
All bleating up to them in panic
And sparkling in scintillant ray—
Beheld a splendor diaphanic—
Effulgence never dawn hath shot,
Nor flying meteors of the night;
And trembling rose, shading the sight;
But heard the angel breathe—Fear not.

So (might one reverently dare
Terrene with heavenly to compare),
So, oft in mid-watch on that sea
Where the ridged Andes of Peru
Are far seen by the coasting crew—
Waves, sails and sailors in accord
Illumed are in a mystery,
Wonder and glory of the Lord,
Though manifest in aspect minor—
Phosphoric ocean in shekinah.

And down now in that dale they go,
Meeting a little St. John boy
In sackcloth shirt and belt of tow,
Leading his sheep. Ever behind
He kept one hand, stained with a shrub,
The which an ewe licked, never coy;
And all the rest with docile mind
Followed; and fleece with fleece did rub.
Beyond, hard by twin planted tents,
Paced as in friendly conference
Two shepherds on the pastoral hill,
Brown patriarchs in shaggy cloak;
Peaceful they went, as in a yoke
The oxen unto pasture oak
To lie in shade when noon is still.
Nibbling the herb, or far or near,
Advanced their flocks, and yet would veer,
For width of range makes wayward will.

Ungar beheld: "What treat they of?
Halving the land?—This might reclaim
Old years of Lot and Abraham
Just ere they parted in remove:
A peaceful parting: 'Let there be
No strife, I pray thee, between me
And thee, my herdmen and thine own;
For we be brethren. See, the land
Is all before thee, fenced by none:
Then separate thyself from me,
I pray thee. If now the left hand
Thou, Lot, wilt take, then I will go
Unto the right; if thou depart
Unto the right, then I will go
Unto the left.'—They parted so,
And not unwisely: both were wise.
'Twas East and West; but North and South!"
Rolfe marked the nip of quivering mouth,

Passion repressed within the eyes;
But ignorance feigned: "This calm," he said,
"How fitly hereabout is shed:
The site of Eden's placed not far;
In bond 'tween man and animal
Survives yet under Asia's star
A link with years before the Fall."
"Indeed," cried Derwent, pleased thereat,
"Blest, blest is here the creature's state
Those pigeons, now, in Saba's hold,
Their wings how winsome would they fold
Alighting at one's feet so soft.
Doves, too, in mosque, I've marked aloft,
At hour of prayer through window come
From trees adjacent, and a 'thrill
Perch, coo, and nestle in the dome,
Or fly with green sprig in the bill.
How by the marble fount in court,
Where for ablution Turks resort
Ere going in to hear the Word,
These small apostles they regard
Which of sweet innocence report.
None stone the dog; caressed, the steed;
Only poor Dobbin (Jew indeed
Of brutes) seems slighted in the East."

Ungar, who chafed in heart of him
At Rolfe's avoidance of his theme
(Although he felt he scarce could blame),
Here turned his vexed mood on the priest:
"As cruel as a Turk: Whence came
That proverb old as the crusades?
From Anglo-Saxons. What are they?
Let the horse answer, and blockades
Of medicine in civil fray!

The Anglo-Saxons—lacking grace
To win the love of any race;
Hated by myriads dispossessed
Of rights—the Indians East and West.
These pirates of the sphere! grave looters—
Grave, canting, Mammonite freebooters,
Who in the name of Christ and Trade
(Oh, bucklered forehead of the brass!)
Deflower the world's last sylvan glade!"
"Alas, alas, ten times alas,
Poor Anglo-Saxons!" Derwent sighed.
"Nay, but if there I lurched too wide,

Respond to this: Old ballads sing
Fair Christian children crucified
By impious Jews: you've heard the thing:
Yes, fable; but there's truth hard by:
How many Hughs of Lincoln, say,
Does Mammon in his mills, to-day,
Crook, if he do not crucify?"
"Ah, come," said Derwent; "come, now, come
Think you that we who build the home
For foundlings, and yield sums immense
To hospitals for indigence "
"Your alms-box, smaller than your till
And poor-house won't absolve your mill.
But what ye are, a straw may tell—
Your dearth of phrases affable.
Italian, French—more tongues than these—
Addresses have of courtesies
In kindliness of man toward man,
By prince used and by artisan,
And not pervertible in sense
Of scorn or slight. Ye have the Sir,
That sole, employed in snub or slur,
Never in pure benevolence,
And at its best a formal term
Of cold regard."
"Ah, why so warm
In mere philology, dear sir?"
Plead Derwent; "there, don't that confer
Sweet amity? I used the word."
But Ungar heeded not—scarce heard
And, earnest as the earnest tomb,
With added feeling, sting, and gloom
His strange impeachment urged. Reply
Came none; they let it go; for why
Argue with man of bitter blood?
But Rolfe he could but grieve within
For countryman in such a mood—
Knowing the cause, the origin.

Canto X - A Monument

Wise Derwent, that discourse to end,
Pointed athwart the dale divine:
"What's yonder object—fountain? shrine?
Companions, let us thither go
And make inspection."

In consent
Silent they follow him in calm.
It proved an ancient monument—
Rude stone; but tablets lent a charm:
Three tablets on three sides. In one
The Tender Shepherd mild looked down
Upon the rescued weanling lost,
Snugged now in arms. In emblem crossed
By pastoral crook, Christ's monogram
(Wrought with a medieval grace)
Showed on the square opposed in face.
But chiefly did they feel the claim
Of the main tablet; there a lamb
On passive haunches upright sate
In patience which reproached not fate;
The two fine furry fore-legs drooping
Like tassels; while the shearer, stooping,
Embraced it with one arm; and all
The fleece rolled off in seamless shawl
Flecked here and there with hinted blood.

It did not shrink; no cry did come:
In still life of that stone subdued
Shearer and shorn alike were dumb.

As with a seventy-four, when lull
Lapses upon the storm, the hull
Rights for the instant, while a moan
Of winds succeeds the howl; so here
In poise of heart and altered tone
With Ungar. Respite brief though dear
It proved; for he: "This type's assigned
To One who sharing not man's mind
Partook man's frame; whose mystic birth
Wrecked him upon this reef of earth
Inclement and inhuman. Yet,
Through all the trials that beset,
He leaned on an upholding arm—
Foreknowing, too, reserves of balm.
But how of them whose souls may claim
Some link with Christ beyond the name,
Which share the fate, but never share
Aid or assurance, and nowhere
Look for requital? Such there be;
In by-lanes o'er the world ye see
The Calvary-faces." All averse
Turned Derwent, murmuring, "Forbear.
Such breakers do the heaven asperse!"

But timely he alert espied,
Upon the mountain humbly kneeling,
Those shepherds twain, while morning-tide
Rolled o'er the hills with golden healing.
It was a rock they kneeled upon,
Convenient for their rite avowed—
Kneeled, and their turbaned foreheads bowed—
Bowed over, till they kissed the stone:
Each shaggy sur-coat heedful spread
For rug, such as in mosque is laid.
About the ledge's favored hem
Mild fed their sheep, enringing them;
While, facing as by second-sight,
Toward Mecca they direct the rite.
"Look; and their backs on Bethlehem turned,"
Cried Rolfe. The priest then, who discerned
The drift, replied, "Yes, for they pray
To Allah. Well, and what of that?
Christ listens, standing in heaven's gate—
Benignant listens, nor doth stay
Upon a syllable in creed:
Vowels and consonants indeed!"
And Rolfe: "But here were Margoth now,
Seeing yon shepherds praying so,
His gibe would run from man to man:
'Which is the humble publican?
Or do they but prostrate them there
To flout you Franks with Islam's prayer?' "
"Doubtless: some shallow thing he'd say,
Poor fellow," Derwent then; "but, nay,
Earnest they are; nor yet they'd part
(If pealed the hour) in street or mart,
From like observance."
"If 'tis so"
The refugee, "let all avow
As openly faith's loyal heart.
By Christians too was God confessed
How frankly! in those days that come
No more to misnamed Christendom!
Religion then was the good guest,
First served, and last, in every gate:
What mottoes upon wall and plate!
She every human venture shared:
The ship in manifest declared
That not disclaiming heaven she thrust
Her bowsprit into fog and storm:
Some current silver bore the palm
Of Christ, token of saint, or bust;

In line devout the pikemen kneeled—
To battle by the rite were sealed.

Men were not lettered, but had sense
Beyond the mean intelligence
That knows to read, and but to read—
Not think. 'Twas harder to mislead
The people then, whose smattering now
Does but the more their ignorance show—
Nay, them to peril more expose—
Is as the ring in the bull's nose
Whereby a pert boy turns and winds
This monster of a million minds.
Men owned true masters; kings owned God—
Their master; Louis plied the rod
Upon himself. In high estate,
Not puffed up like a democrat
In office, how with Charlemagne?
Look up he did, look up in reign—
Humbly look up, who might look down:
His meekest thing was still his crown:
How meek on him; since, graven there,
Among the Apostles twelve behold,
Stern Scriptural precepts were enrolled,
High admonitions, meet for kings.
The coronation was a prayer,
Which yet in ceremonial clings.
The church was like a bonfire warm:
All ranks were gathered round the charm."
Derwent, who vainly had essayed
To impede the speaker, or blockade,
Snatched at the bridle here: "Ho, wait;
A word, impetuous laureate!
This bric-a-brac-ish style (outgrown
Almost, where first it gave the tone)
Of lauding the quaint ages old—
But nay, that's satire; I withhold.
Grant your side of the shield part true:
What then? why, turn the other: view
The buckler in reverse. Don't sages
Denominate those times Dark Ages?
Dark Middle Ages, time's midnight!"
"If night, it was no starless one;
Art still admires what then was done:
A strength they showed which is of light.
Not more the Phidian marbles prove
The graces of the Grecian prime
And indicate what men they were,

Than the grand minsters in remove
Do intimate, if not declare
A magnanimity which our time
Would envy, were it great enough
To comprehend. Your counterbuff,
However, holds. Yes, frankly, yes,
Another side there is, admit.

Nor less the very worst of it
Reveals not such a shamelessness
Of evildoer and hypocrite,
And sordid mercenary sin
As these days vaunt and revel in."
"No use, no use," the priest aside;
"Patience! it is the maddest tide;"
And seated him.
And Ungar then:
"What's overtaken ye pale men?
Shrewd are ye, the main chance ye heed:
Has God quite lost his throne indeed
That lukewarm now ye grow? Wilt own,
Council ye take with fossil-stone?
Your sects do nowadays create
Churches as worldly as the state.
And, for your more established forms—
Ah, once in York I viewed through storms
The Minster's majesty of mien—
Towers, peaks, and pinnacles sublime—
Faith's iceberg, stranded on a scene
How alien, and an alien time;
But now"—he checked himself, and stood.

Whence this strange bias of his mood
(Thought they) leaning to things corroded,
By many deemed for aye exploded?
But, truly, knowing not the man,
At fault they in conjecture ran.
But Ungar (as in fitter place
Set down) being sprung from Romish race,
Albeit himself had spared to feed
On any one elected creed
Or rite, though much he might recall
In annals bearing upon all;
And, in this land named of Behest,
A wandering Ishmael from the West;
Inherited the Latin mind,
Which latc blown by the adverse wind
Of harder fortunes that molest—

Kindled from ember into coal.

The priest, as one who keeps him whole,
Anew turns toward the kneeling twain:
"Your error's slight, or, if a stain,
'Twill fade. Our Lord enjoins good deeds
Nor catechiseth in the creeds."
A something in the voice or man,
Or in assumption of the turn
Which prior theme did so adjourn,
Pricked Ungar, and a look he ran
Toward Derwent—an electric light
Chastising in its fierce revolt;
Then settled into that still night
Of cloud which has discharged the bolt.

Canto XI - Disquiet

At breakfast in refectory there
The priest—if Clarel not mistook—
The good priest wore the troubled air
Of honest heart striving to brook
Injury, which from words abstained,
And, hence, not readily arraigned;
Which to requite in its own sort
Is not allowed in heaven's high court,
Or self-respect's. Such would forget,
But for the teasing doubt or fret
Lest unto worldly witness mere
The injury none the less appear
To challenge notice at the least.

Ungar withdrew, leaving the priest
Less ill at ease; who now a thought
Threw out, as 'twere in sad concern
For one whose nature, sour or stern,
Still dealt in all unhandsome flings

At happy times and happy things:
" 'The bramble sayeth it is naught:'
Poor man!" But that; and quite forbore
To vent his grievance. Nor less sore
He felt it—Clarel so inferred,
Recalling here too Mortmain's word
Of cutting censorship. How then?
While most who met him frank averred

That Derwent ranked with best of men,
The Swede and refugee unite
In one repugnance, yea, and slight.
How take, construe their ill-content?
A thing of vein and temperament?
Rolfe liked him; and if Vine said naught,
Yet even Vine seemed not uncheered
By fair address. Then stole the thought
Of how the priest had late appeared
In that one confidential hour,
Ambiguous on Saba's tower.
There he dismissed it, let it fall:
To probe overmuch seems finical.
Nor less (for still the point did tease,
Nor would away and leave at ease),
Nor less, I wonder, if ere long
He'll turn this off, not worth a song,
As lightly as of late he turned
Poor Mortmain's sally when he burned?

Canto XII - Of Pope and Turk

Marking the priest not all sedate,
Rolfe, that a friend might fret discard,
Turned his attention to debate
Between two strangers at the board.
In furtherance of his point or plea
One said:
"Late it was told to me,
And by the man himself concerned,
A merchant Frank on Syria's coast,
That in a fire which traveled post,
His books and records being burned,
His Christian debtors held their peace;
The Islam ones disclaimed release,
And came with purses and accounts."
"And duly rendered their amounts?
'Twas very kind. But oh, the greed,
Rapacity, and crime at need
In satraps which oppress the throng."
"True. But with these 'tis, after all,
Wrong-doing purely personal—
Not legislated—not a wrong
Law-sanctioned. No: the Turk, admit,
In scheme of state, the scheme of it,
Upon the civil arm confers

A sway above the scimeter's—
The civil power itself subjects
Unto that Koran which respects
Nor place nor person. Nay, adjourn
The jeer; for now aside we'll turn.
Dismembered Poland and her throe
In Ninety-Five, all unredressed:
Did France, did England then protest?"
"England? I'm sure I do not know.
Come, I distrust your shifting so.
Pray, to what end now is this pressed?"
"Why, here armed Christendom looking on,
In protest the Sultan stood alone."
"Indeed? But all this, seems to me,
Savors of Urquhart's vanity."
"The commentator on the East?"
"The same: that very inexact
Eccentric ideologist
Now obsolete."
"And that's your view?
He stands for God."
"I stand by fact."
"Well then, another fact or two;
When Poland's place in Thirty-One
Was blotted out, the Turk again
Protested, with one other man,
The Pope; these, and but these alone;
And in the protest both avowed
'Twas made for justice's sake and God.—
You smile."
"Oh no: but very clear
The protest prompted was by fear
In Turk and Pope, that time might come
When spoliation should drive home
Upon themselves. Besides, you know
The Polish church was Catholic:
The Czar would wrest it to the Greek:
'Twas that touched Rome. But let it go.—
In pith, what is it you would show?
Are Turks our betters? Very strange
Heaven's favor does not choicely range
Upon these Islam people good:
Bed-rid they are, behindhand all,
While Europe flowers in plenitude
Of wealth and commerce."
"I recall
Nothing in Testament which saith
That worldliness shall not succeed

In that wherein it laboreth.

Howbeit, the Sultan's coming on:
Fine lesson from ye has he won
Of late; apt pupil he indeed:
Ormus, that riches did confer,
Ormus is made a borrower:
Selim, who grandly turbaned sat,
Verges on bankruptcy and—hat.
But this don't touch the rank and file;
At least, as yet. But preach and work:
You'll civilize the barbarous Turk—
Nay, all the East may reconcile:
That done, let Mammon take the wings of even,
And mount and civilize the saints in heaven."

"I laugh—I like a brave caprice!
And, sir "
But here did Rolfe release
His ear, and Derwent too. A stir
In court was heard of man and steed—
Neighings and mountings, din indeed
And Rolfe: "Come, come; our traveler."

Canto XIII - The Church of the Star

They rise, and for a little space
In farewell Agath they detain,
Transferred here to a timelier train
Than theirs. A work-day, passive face
He turns to Derwent's Luck to thee!
No slight he means—'tis far from that
But, schooled by the inhuman sea,
He feels 'tis vain to wave the hat
In God-speed on this mortal strand;
Recalling all the sailing crews
Destined to sleep in ocean sand,
Cheered from the wharf with blithe adieus.
Nor less the heart's farewell they say,
And bless the old man on his way.

Led by a slender monk and young,
With curls that ringed the shaven crown,
Courts now and shrines they trace. That thong
Ascetic which can life chastise
Down to her bleak necessities,

They mark in coarse serge of his gown,
And girdling rope, with cross of wood
For tag at end; and hut-like hood
Superfluous now behind him thrown;
And sandals which expose the skin
Transparent, and the blue vein thin
Meandering there: the feet, the face
Alike in lucid marble grace.

His simple manners self-possessed
Both saint and noble-born suggest;
Yet under quietude they mark
The slumbering of a vivid spark—
Excitable, if brought to test.
A Tuscan, he exchanged the charm
Val d'Arno yields, for this dull calm
Of desert. Was his youth self-given
In frank oblation unto heaven?
Or what inducement might disarm
This Isaac when too young to know?

Hereon they, pacing, musc till, lo,
The temple opens in dusk glades
Of long-drawn double colonnades:
Monoliths two-score and eight.
Rolfe looked about him, pleased in state:
"But this is goodly! Here we rove
As down the deep Dodona grove:
Years, years and years these boles have stood!—
Late by the spring in idle mood
My will I made (if ye recall),
Providing for the Inn of Trees:
But ah, to set out trunks like these
In harbor open unto all
For generations!" So in vein
Rolfe free descanted as through fane
They passed. But noting now the guide
In acquiescence by their side,
He checked himself: "Why prate I here?
This brother—I usurp his sphere."

They came unto a silver star
In pavement set which none do mar
By treading. Here at pause remained
The monk; till, seeing Rolfe refrained,
And all, from words, he said: "The place,
Signori, where that shining grace
Which led the Magi, stood; below,

The Manger is." They comment none
Not voicing everything they know,
In cirque about that silver star
They quietly gaze thereupon.
But, turning now, one glanced afar
Along the columned aisles, and thought
Of Baldwin whom the mailed knights brought
While Godfrey's requiem did ring,
Hither to Bethlehem, and crowned
His temples helmet-worn, with round
Of gold and velvet—crowned him king—
King of Jerusalem, on floor
Of this same nave august, above
The Manger in its low remove
Where lay, a thousand years before,
The Child of awful worshiping,
Destined to prove all slights and scorns
And a God's coronation—thorns.
Not Derwent's was that revery;
Another thing his heart possessed,
The clashing of the East and West,
Odd sense of incongruity;
He felt a secret impulse move
To start a humorous comment slant
Upon the monk, and sly reprove.
But no: I'll curb the Protestant
And modern in me—at least here
For time I'll curb it. Perish truth
If it but act the boor, in sooth,
Requiting courtesy with jeer;
For courteous is our guide, with grace
Of a pure heart.
Some little trace,
May be, of Derwent's passing thought
The Tuscan from his aspect caught;
And turned him: "Pardon! but the crypt:
This way, signori—follow me."
Down by a rock-hewn stair they slipped,
Turning by steps which winding be,

Winning a sparry chamber brave
Unsearched by that prose critic keen,
The daylight. Archimago's cave
Was here? or that more sorcerous scene
The Persian Sibyl kept within
For turbaned musings? Bowing o'er,
Crossing himself, and on the knee,
Straight did the guide that grot adore;

Then, rising, and as one set free:
"The place of the Nativity."
Dim pendent lamps, in cluster small
Were Pleiads of the mystic hall;
Fair lamps of silver, lamps of gold—
Rich gifts devout of monarchs old,
Kings catholic. Rare objects beamed
All round, recalling things but dreamed:
Solomon's talismans garnered up,
His sword, his signet-ring and cup.
In further caverns, part revealed,
What silent shapes like statues kneeled;
What brown monks moved by twinkling shrines
Like Aztecs down in silver mines.

This, this the Stable mean and poor?
Noting their looks, to ward surprise,
The Italian: "'Tis incrusted o'er
With marbles, so that now one's eyes
Meet not the natural wall. This floor "
"But how? within a cave we stand!"
"Yes, caves of old to use were put
For cattle, and with gates were shut.
One meets them still—with arms at hand,
The keepers nigh. Sure it need be
That if in Gihon ye have been,
Or hereabouts, yourselves have seen
The grots in question."
They agree;
And silent in their hearts confess
The strangeness, but the truth no less.

Anew the guide: "Ere now we get
Further herein, indulge me yet;"
But paused awhile: "Though o'er this cave,
Where Christ" (and crossed himself) "had birth,
Constantine's mother reared the Nave
Whose Greek mosaics fade in bloom,
No older church in Christendom;
And generations, with the girth
Of domes and walls, have still enlarged
And built about; yet convents, shrines,
Cloisters and towers, take not for signs,
Entreat ye, of meek faith submerged
Under proud masses. Be it urged
As all began from these small bounds,
So, by all avenues and gates,
All here returns, hereto redounds:

In this one Cave all terminates:
In honor of the Manger sole
Saints, kings, knights, prelates reared the whole."
He warmed. Ah, fervor bought too dear:
The fingers clutching rope and cross;
Life too intense; the cheek austere
Deepening in hollow, waste and loss.
They marked him; and at heart some knew
Inklings they loved not to pursue.
But Rolfe recalled in fleeting gleam
The first Franciscan, richly born—
The youthful one who, night and morn,
In Umbria ranged the hills in dream,
And first devised the girdling cord
In type that rebel senses so
Should led be led like beast abroad
By halter. Tuscan! in the glow
And white light of thy faith's illumings,
In vigils, fervent prayers and trances,
Agonies and self-consumings—
Renewest thou the young Saint Francis?
So inly Rolfe; when, in low tone
Considerate Derwent whispered near:
"'Tis doubtless the poor boy's first year
In Bethlehem; time will abate
This novice-ardor; yes, sedate
He'll grow, adapt him to the sphere."

Close to the Sanctum now they drew,
A semicircular recess;
And there, in marble floor, they view
A silver sun which (friars profess)
Is set in plummet-line exact
Beneath the star in pavement-tract
Above; and raying from this sun
Shoot jasper-spikes, which so point out
Argent inscription roundabout
In Latin text; which thus may run:
THE VIRGIN HERE BROUGHT FORTH THE SON.
The Tuscan bowed him; then with air
Friendly he turned; but something there
In Derwent's look—no matter what—
An open levity 'twas not—
Disturbed him; and in accents clear,
As challenged in his faith sincere:
"I trust tradition! Here He lay
Who shed on Mary's breasts the ray:
SaltJator Mundi!"

Turning now,

He noted, and he bade them see
Where, with a timid piety
A band of rustics bent them low
In worship mute: "Shepherds these are,
And come from pastoral hills not far
Whereon they keep the night-watch wild:
These, like their sires, adore the CHILD,
And in same spot. But, mixed with these,
Mark ye yon poor swart images
In other garb? But late they fled
From over Jordan hither; yes,
Escaping so the heinousness
Of one with price upon his head.

But look, and yet seem not to peer,
Lest pain ye give: an eye, an ear,
A hand, is mutilate or gone:
The mangler marked them for his own
But Christ redeems them." Derwent here
His eyes withdrew, but Ungar not
While visibly the red blood shot
Into his thin-skinned scar, and sent
As seemed, a pulse of argument
Confirming so some angry sense
Of evil, and malevolence
In man toward man.
Now, lower down
The cave, the Manger they descry
With marble lined; and, o'er it thrown,
A lustrous saint-cloth meets the eye.
And suits of saint-cloths here they have
Wherewith to deck the Manger brave:
Gifts of the Latin princes, these—
Fair Christmas gifts, these draperies.
A damask one of gold and white
Rich flowered with pinks embroidered bright
Was for the present week in turn
The adornment of the sacred Urn.
Impressive was it here to note
Those herdsmen in the shaggy coat:
Impressive, yet partook of dream;
It touched the pilgrims, as might seem;
Which pleased the monk; but in disguise
Modest he dropped his damsel-eyes.
Thought Derwent then: Demure in sooth!
'Tis like a maid in lily of youth

Who grieves not in her core of glee
By spells of grave virginity
To cozen men to foolish looks
While she—who reads such hearts' hid nooks?—
What now? "Signori, here, believe
Where night and day, while ages run
Faith in these lamps burns on and on
'Tis good to spend one's Christmas Eve;
Yea, better rather than in land
Which may your holly tree command,
And greens profuse which ye inweave.

Canto XIV - Soldier and Monk

Fervid he spake. And Ungar there
Appeared (if looks allow surmise)
In latent way to sympathize,
Yet wonder at the votary's air;
And frequent too he turned his face
To note the grotto, and compare
These haunted precincts with the guide,
As so to realize the place,
Or fact from fable to divide;
At times his changeful aspect wore
Touch of the look the simple shepherds bore.
  The Tuscan marked; he pierced him through,
Yet gently, gifted with the clew—
Ascetic insight; and he caught
The lapse within the soldier's thought,
The favorable frame, nor missed
Appealing to it, to enlist
Or influence, or drop a seed
Which might some latter harvest breed.
Gently approaching him, he said:
"True sign you bear: your sword's a cross."
Ungar but started, as at loss
To take the meaning, and yet led
To marvel how that mannered word
Did somehow slip into accord
With visitings that scarce might cleave
Shadows, but shadows fugitive.
He lifted up the steel: the blade
Was straight; the hilt, a bar: "'Tis true;
A cross, it is a cross," he said;
And touched seemed, though 'twas hardly new.

When glowed the other; and, again:
Ignatlus was a soldier too,
And Martin. 'Tis the pure disdain
Of life, or, holding life the real,
Still subject to a brave ideal—
'Tis this that makes the tent a porch
Whereby the warrior wins the church:
The habit of renouncing, yes,
'Tis good, a good preparedness.—
Our founder"—here he raised his eyes
As unto all the sanctities—
"Footing it near Rieti town
Met a young knight on horseback, one
Named Angelo Tancredi: 'Lo,'
He said, 'Thy belt thou'lt change for cord
Thy spurs for mire, good Angelo,
And be a true knight of the Lord.'
And he, the cavalier " Aside
A brother of the cowl here drew
This ardent proselyting guide,
Detaining him in interview
About some matter. Ungar stood
Lost in his thoughts.
In neighborhood
Derwent by Rolfe here chanced to bide
And said: "It just occurs to me
As interesting in its way,
That these Franciscans steadily
Have been custodians of the Tomb
And Manger, ever since the day
Of rescue under Godfrey's plume
Long centuries ago." Rolfe said:
"Ay; and appropriate seems it too
For the Franciscan retinue
To keep these places, since their head,
St. Francis, spite his scouted hood
May claim more of similitude
To Christ, than any man we know.
Through clouds of myth investing him—
Obscuring, yet attesting him,
He burns with the seraphic glow
And perfume of a holy flower.
Sweetness, simplicity, with power!
By love's true miracle of charm
He instituted a reform
(Not insurrection) which restored
For time the spirit of his Lord
On earth. If sad perversion came

Unto his order—what of that?
All Christianity shares the same:
Pure things men need adulterate
And so adapt them to the kind."
"Oh, oh! But I have grown resigned
To these vagaries.—And for him,
Assisi's saint—a good young man,
No doubt, and beautiful to limn;
Yes, something soft, Elysian;
Nay, rather, the transparent hue
Unearthly of a maiden tranced
In sleep somnambulic; no true
Color of health; beauty enhanced
To enervation. In a word,
For all his charity divine,
Love, self-devotion, ardor fine—
Unmanly seems he!"
"Of our Lord
The same was said by Machiavel,
Or hinted, rather. Prithee, tell,
What is it to be manly?"
"Why,
To be man-like"—and here the chest
Bold out he threw—"man at his best!"
"But even at best, one might reply,
Man is that thing of sad renown
Which moved a deity to come down
And save him. Lay not too much stress
Upon the carnal manliness:
The Christliness is better—higher;
And Francis owned it, the first friar.
Too orthodox is that?"
"See, see,"
Said Derwent, with kind air of one
Who would a brother's weak spot shun:
"Mark this most delicate drapery;
If woven by some royal dame—
God bless her and her tambour frame!"

Canto XV - Symphonies

Meanwhile with Vine there, Clarel stood
Aside in friendly neighborhood,
And felt a flattering pleasure stir
At words—nor in equivocal tone
Freakish, or leaving to infer,

Such as beforetime he had known—
Breathed now by that exceptional one
In unconstraint:
"'Tis very much
The cold fastidious heart to touch
This way; nor is it mere address
That so could move one's silver chord.
How he transfigured Ungar's sword!
Delusive is this earnestness
Which holds him in its passion pale—
Tenant of melancholy's dale
Of mirage? To interpret him,
Perhaps it needs a swallow-skim
Over distant time. Migrate with me
Across the years, across the sea.—
How like a Poor Clare in her cheer
(Grave Sister of his order sad)
Showed nature to that Cordelier
Who, roving in the Mexic glade,
Saw in a bud of happy dower
Whose stalk entwined the tropic tree,
Emblems of Christ's last agony:
In anthers, style, and fibers torn,
The five wounds, nails, and crown of thorn;
And named it so the passion-flower.
What beauty in that sad conceit!
Such charm, the title still we meet.
Our guide, methinks, where'er he turns
For him this passion-flower burns;
And all the world is elegy.
A green knoll is to you and me
But pastoral, and little more:
To him 'tis even Calvary
Where feeds the Lamb. This passion-flower—
But list!"
Hid organ-pipes unclose
A timid rill of slender sound,
Which gains in volume—grows, and flows
Gladsome in amplitude of bound.
Low murmurs creep. From either side
Tenor and treble interpose,
And talk across the expanding tide:
Debate, which in confusion merges—
Din and clamor, discord's hight:
Countering surges—paeans—dirges—
Mocks, and laughter light.
But rolled in long ground-swell persistent,
A tone, an under-tone assails

And overpowers all near and distant;
Earnest and sternest, it prevails.
Then terror, horror—wind and rain—
Accents of undetermined fear,
And voices as in shipwreck drear:
A sea, a sea of spirits in pain!
The suppliant cries decrease—
The voices in their ferment cease:
One wave rolls over all and whelms to peace.

But hark—oh, hark!
Whence, whence this stir, this whirr of wings?
Numbers numberless convening—
Harps and child-like carolings
In happy holiday of meaning:
To God be glory in the hight,
For tidings glad we bring;
Good will to men, and peace on earth
We children-cherubs sing!

To God be glory in the depth,
As in the hight be praise;
He who shall break the gates of death
A babe in manger rays.

Ye people all in every land,
Embrace, embrace, be kin:
Immanuel's born in Bethlehem,
And gracious years begin!

It dies; and, half around the heavenly sphere,
Like silvery lances lightly touched aloft—
Like Northern Lights appealing to the ear,
An elfin melody chimes low and soft.
That also dies, that last strange fairy-thrill:
Slowly it dies away, and all is sweetly still.

Canto XVI - The Convent Roof

To branching grottoes next they fare,
Old caves of penitence and prayer,
Where Paula kneeled—her urn is there—
Paula the Widow, Scipio's heir
But Christ's adopted. Well her tomb
Adjoins her friend's, renowned Jerome.
Never the attending Druze resigned

His temperate poise, his moderate mind;
While Belex, in punctilious guard,
Relinquished not the martial ward:
"If by His tomb hot strife may be,
Trust ye His cradle shall be free?
Heed one experienced, sirs." His sword,
Held cavalier by jingling chain,
Dropping at whiles, would clank amain
Upon the pave.
"I pray ye now,"
To him said Rolfe in accents low,
"Have care; for see ye not ye jar
These devotees? they turn—they cease
(Hearing your clanging scimeter)
Their suppliance to the Prince of Peace."

Like miners from the shaft, or tars
From forth the hold, up from those spars
And grottoes, by the stony stair
They climb, emerge, and seek the air
In open space.
"Save me, what now?"
Cried Derwent, foremost of the group—
"The holy water!"
Hanging low
Outside, was fixed a scalloped stoup
Or marble shell, to hold the wave
Of Jordan, for true ones to lave
The finger, and so make the sign,
The Cross's sign, ere in they slip
And bend the knee. In this divine
Recess, deliberately a lip
Was lapping slow, with long-drawn pains,
The liquid globules, last remains
Of the full stone. Astray, alas,
Athirst and lazed, it was—the ass;
The friars, withdrawn for time, having left
That court untended and bereft.
"Was ever Saracen so bold!"
"Well, things have come to pretty pass—
The mysteries slobbered by an ass!"
"Mere Nature do we here behold?"
So they. But he, the earnest guide,
Turning the truant there aside,
Said, and in unaffected tone:
"What should it know, this foolish one?
It is an infidel we see:
Ah, the poor brute's stupidity!"

"I hardly think so," Derwent said;
"For, look, it hangs the conseious head."
The friar no relish had for wit,
No sense, perhaps, too rapt for it,
Pre-occupied. So, having seen
The ass led back, he bade adieu;
But first, and with the kindliest mien:
"Signori, would ye have fair view
Of Bethlehem of Judaea, pray
Ascend to roof: ye take yon stair.
And now, heaven have ye in its care—
Me save from sin, and all from error!
Farewell."—But Derwent: "Yet delay:
Fain would we cherish when away:
Thy name, then?" "Brother Salvaterra."
"'Tis a fair name. And, brother, we
Are not insensible, conceive,
To thy most Christian courtesy.—
He goes. Sweet echo does he leave
In Salvaterra: may it dwell!
Silver in every syllable!"
"And import too," said Rolfe.
They fare
And win the designated stair,
And climb; and, as they climb, in bell
Of Derwent's repetition, fell:
"Me save from sin, and all from error!
So prays good brother Salvaterra."

In paved flat roof, how ample there,
They tread a goodly St. Mark's Square
Aloft. An elder brother lorn
They meet, with shrunken cheek, and worn
Like to a slab whereon may weep
The unceasing water-drops. And deep
Within his hollow gown-sleeves old
His viewless hands he did enfold.
He never spake, but moved away
With shuffling pace of dragged infirm delay.
"Seaward he gazed," said Rolfe, "toward home:
An empty longing!"
"Cruel Rome!"
Sighed Derwent; "See, though, good to greet
The vale of eclogue, Boaz' seat.
Trips Ruth there, yonder?" thitherward
Down pointing where the vineyards meet.
At that dear name in Bethlehem heard,
How Clarel starts. Not Agar's child—

Naomi's! Then, unreconciled,
And in reaction falling low,
He saw the files Armenian go,
The tapers round the virgin's bier,
And heard the boys' light strophe free
Overborne by the men's antistrophe.
Illusion! yet he knew a fear:
"Fixed that this second night we bide
In Bethlehem?" he asked aside.
Yes, so 'twas planned. For moment there
He thought to leave them and repair
Alone forthwith to Salem. Nay,
Doubt had unhinged so, that her sway,
In minor things even, could retard
The will and purpose. And, beyond,
Prevailed the tacit pilgrim-bond—
Of no slight force in his regard;
Besides, a diffidence was sown:
None knew his heart, nor might he own;
And, last, feared he to prove the fear?
With outward things he sought to clear
His mind; and turned to list the tone
Of Derwent, who to Rolfe: "Here now
One stands emancipated."
                    "yow?"
"The air—the air, the liberal air!
Those witcheries of the cave ill fare
Reviewed aloft. Ah, Salvaterra,
So winning in thy dulcet error—
How fervid thou! Nor less thy tone,
So heartfelt in sincere effusion,
Is hardly that more chastened one
We Protestants feel. But the illusion!
Those grottoes: yes, void now they seem
As phantoms which accost in dream—
Accost and fade. Hold you with me?"
"Yes, partly: I in part agree.
In Kedron too, thou mayst recall,
The monkish night of festival,
And masque enacted—how it shrank
When, afterward, in nature frank,
Upon the terrace thrown at ease,
Like magi of the old Chalda-a,
Viewing Rigel and Betelguese,
We breathed the balm-wind from Saba-a.
All shows and forms in Kedron had—
Nor hymn nor banner made them glad
To me. And yet—why, who may know!

These things come down from long ago.
While so much else partakes decay,
While states, tongues, manners pass away,
How wonderful the Latin rite
Surviving still like oak austere
Over crops rotated year by year,
Or Caesar's tower on London's site.
But, tell me: stands it true in fact
That robe and ritual—every kind
By Rome employed in ways exact—
However strange to modern mind,
Or even absurd (like cards Chinese
In ceremonial usages),
Not less of faith or need were born—
Survive untampered with, unshorn;
Date far back to a primal day,
Obscure and hard to trace indeed—
The springing of the planted seed
In the church's first organic sway?
Still for a type, a type or use,
Each decoration so profuse
Budding and flowering? Tell me here."
"If but one could! To be sincere,
Rome's wide campania of old lore
Ecclesiastic—that waste shore
I've shunned: an instinct makes one fear
Malarial places. But I'll tell
That at the mass this very morn
I marked the broidered maniple
Which by the ministrant was worn:
How like a napkin does it show,
Thought I, a napkin on the arm
Of servitor. And hence we know
Its origin. In the first days
(And who denies their simple charm!)
When the church's were like household ways,
Some served the flock in humble state
At Eucharist, passed cup or plate.
The thing of simple use, you see,
Tricked out—embellished—has become
Theatric and a form. There's Rome!
Yet what of this, since happily
Each superflux men now disown."
"Perchance!—'Tis an ambiguous time;
And periods unforecast come on.
Recurs to me a Persian rhyme:
In Pera late an Asian man,
With stately cap of Astracan,

I knew in arbored coffee-house
On bluff above the Bosphorus.
Strange lore was his, and Saadi's wit:
Over pipe and Mocha long we'd sit
Discussing themes which thrive in shade.
In pause of talk a way he had
Of humming a low air of his:
I asked him once, What trills your bird?
And he recited it in word,
To pleasure me, and this it is:
"Flamen, flamen, put away
Robe and mitre glorious:
Doubt undeifies the day!
Look, in vapors odorous
As the spice-king's funeral-pyre,
Dies the Zoroastrian fire
On your altars in decay:
The rule, the Magian rule is run,
And Mythra abdicates the sun!"

Canto XVII - A Transition

"Fine, very fine," said Derwent light;
"But, look, yon rustics there in sight
Crossing the slope; and are they not
Those Arabs that we saw in grot?"
"Why, who they be their garb bespeaks:
Yes, 'tis those Arab Catholics."
"Catholic Arabs? Say not that!
Some words don't chime together, see.'
"Oh, never mind the euphony:
We saw them worship, and but late.
Our Bethlehemites, the guard, they too
Are Catholics. I talked with one,
And much from his discourse I drew,
Which the conventicles would shun:
These be the children of the sun:
They like not prosing—turn the lip
From Luther's jug—prefer to sip
From that tall chalice brimmed with wine
Which Rome hath graved, and made to shine
For haughty West and barbarous East,
To win all people to her feast."
"So, so! But, glamoured in that school
Of taking shows and charmful rites,
What ween they of Christ's genuine rule,

These credulous poor neophytes?
Alas for such disciples! No,
At mass before the altar, own,
The celebrant in mystic gown
To them is but a Prospero,
A prince of magic. I deplore
That zeal in such conversions seeks
Less Christians than good Catholics:
And here one might append much more.
But drop.—Yon vineyards they are fair.
For hill-side scenery—for curve
Of beauty in a meek reserve—
'Tis Bethlehem the bell may bear!"
Longer he gazed, then turned aside.

Clarel was left with Rolfe. In view
Leaned Ungar, watching there the guide
Below, who passed on errand new.
"Your judgment of him let me crave—
Him there," here lowly Rolfe.
"I would
I were his mate," in earnest mood
Clarel rejoined; "such faith to have,
I'd take the rest, even Crib and Cave.

"Ah, you mistake me; him I mean,
Our comrade, Ungar."
"He? at loss
I am: at loss, for he's most strange;
Wild, too, adventurous in range;
And suffers; so that one might glean
An added import from the word
The Tuscan spake: You bear a cross,
Referring to the straight-hilt sword."
"I know. And when the Arnaut ran,
But yesterday, with arms how bright
(Like wheeling Phcebus flashing light),
Superb about this sombrous man—
A soldier too with vouching tinge;
Methought, O War, thy bullion fringe
Never shall gladsome make thy pall.
Ungar is Mars in funeral
Of reminiscence—not in pledge
And glory of brave equipage
And manifesto. But some keen
Side-talk I had with him yestreen:
Brave soldier and stout thinker both;
In this regard, and in degree,

An Ethan Allen, by my troth,
Or Herbert lord of Cherbury,
Dusked over. 'Tis an iron glove,
An armed man in the Druid grove."

Canto XVIII - The Hill-Side

Pertaining unto nations three—
Or, rather, each unto its clan—
Greek, Latin, and Armenian,
About the fane three convents be.
Confederate on the mountain fair,
Blunt buttressed huge with masonry,
They mass an Ehrenbreitstein there.
In these, and in the Empress' fane
Enough they gather to detain
Or occupy till afternoon;
When some of them the ridge went down
To view that legendary grot
Whose milky chalkiness of vest
Derived is (so the hinds allot)
From droppings of Madonna's breast:
A fairy tale: yet, grant it, due
To that creative love alone
Wherefrom the faun and cherub grew,
With genii good and Oberon.

Returning, part way up the hight,
Ungar they met; and Vine in sight.

Here all repose them.
"Look away,
Cried Derwent, westward pointing; —see,
How glorified yon vapors be!
It is the dying of the day;
A hopeful death-bed: yes, need own
There is a morrow for the sun."

So, mild they sat in pleased delay.
Vine turned—what seemed a random word
Shyly let fall; and they were stirred
Thereby to broach anew the theme—
How wrought the sites of Bethlehem
On Western natures. Here some speech
Was had; and then: "For me," Rolfe said,
"From Bethlehem here my musings reach

Yes—frankly—to Tahiti's beach."
"Tahiti?" Derwent; "you have sped!"
"Ay, truant humor. But to me
That vine-wreathed urn of Ver, in sea
Of halcyons, where no tides do flow
Or ebb, but waves bide peacefully
At brim, by beach where palm trees grow
That sheltered Omai's olive race—
Tahiti should have been the place
For Christ in advent."
                         "Deem ye so?
Or on the topic's budding bough
But lights your fancy's robin?"
                                 "Nay, "
Said Ungar, "err one if he say
The God's design was, part, to broach
Rebuke of man's factitious life;
So, for his first point of approach,
Came thereunto where that was rife,
The land of Pharisees and scorn—
Juda-a, with customs hard as horn."
This, chief, to Rolfe and Derwent twain.
But Derwent, if no grudge he knew,
Still felt some twinges of the pain
(Vibrations of the residue)
That morning in the dale incurred;
Wherefore, at present he abstained
When Ungar spake, from any word
Receptive. Rolfe reply maintained;
And much here followed, though of kind
Scarce welcome to the priest. Resigned
He heard; till, at a hint, the Cave
He named:
            "If on the first review
Its shrines seemed each a gilded grave
Yet, reconsidered, they renew
The spell of the transmitted story—
The grace, the innocence, the glory:
Shepherds, the Manger, and the CHILD:
What wonder that it has beguiled
So many generations! Ah,
Though much we knew in desert late
Beneath no kind auspicious star,
Of lifted minds in poised debate—
'Twas of the brain. Consult the heart!
Spouse to the brain—can coax or thwart:
Does she renounce the trust divine?
Hide it she may, but scarce resign;

Like to a casket buried deep
Which, in a fine and fibrous throng,
The rootlets of the forest keep—
'Tis tangled in her meshes strong."
"Yes, yes," cried Rolfe; "that tone delights;
But oh, these legends, relics, sites!
Of yore, you know, Greeks showed the place
Where Argo landed, and the stone
That served to anchor Argo; yes,
And Agamemnon's scepter, throne;
Mars' spear; and so on. More to please,
Where the goddess suckled Hercules—
Priests showed that spot, a sacred one."
"Well then, Madonna's but a dream,
The Manger and the Crib. So deem:

So be it; but undo it! Nay,
Little avails what sages say:
Tell Romeo that Juliet's eyes
Are chemical; e'en analyze
The iris; show 'tis albumen—
Gluten—fish jelly mere. What then?
To Romeo it is still love's sky:
He loves: enough! Though Faith no doubt
Seem insubstantial as a sigh,
Never ween that 'tis a water-spout
Dissolving, dropping into dew
At pistol-shot. Besides, review
That comprehensive Christian scheme:
It catches man at each extreme:
Simple august; strange as a dream,
Yet practical as plodding life:
Not use and sentiment at strife."
They hearken: none aver dissent,
Nor one confirms him; while his look
Unwitting an expression took,
Scarce insincere, yet so it lent
Provocative to Ungar's heart;
Who, bridling the embittered part,
Thus spake: "This yieldeth no content:
Your implication lacketh stay:
There is a callousness in clay.

Christ's pastoral parables divine,
Breathing the sweet breath of sweet kine,
As wholesome too; how many feel?
Feel! rather put it—comprehend?
Not unto all does nature lend

The gift; at hight such love's appeal
Is hard to know, as in her deep
Is hate; a prior love must steep
The spirit; head nor heart have marge
Commensurate in man at large."
"Indulge me," Derwent; "Grant it so
As you present it; 'tis most strange
How Christ could work his powerful change:
The world turned Christian long ago."
"The world but joined the Creed Divine
With prosperous days and Constantine;
The world turned Christian, need confess,
But the world remained the world, no less:
The world turned Christian: where's the odds?
Hearts change not in the change of gods.
Despite professions, outward shows—
So far as working practice goes,
More minds with shrewd Voltaire have part
Than now own Jesus in the heart. "
"Not rashly judge," said Derwent grave;
"Prudence will here decision waive."
"No: shift the test. How Buddha pined!
Pierced with the sense of all we bear,
Not only ills by fate assigned,
But misrule of our selfish mind,
Fain would the tender sage repair.
Well, Asia owns him. But the lives:
Buddha but in a name survives—
A name, a rite. Confucius, too:
Does China take his honest hue?
Some forms they keep, some forms of his;
But well we know them, the Chinese.
Ah, Moses, thy deterring dart!—
Etherial visitants of earth,
Foiled benefactors, proves your worth
But sundry texts, disowned in mart,
Light scratched, not graved on man's hard heart?
'Tis penalty makes sinners start."

Canto XIX - A New-Comer

"Good echoes, echo it! Ho, chant,
'Tis penalty we sinners want:
By all means, penalty!"
What man
Thus struck in here so consonant?

They turn them, and a stranger scan.
As through the rigging of some port
Where cheek by jowl the ships resort—
The sea-beat hulls of briny oak—
Peereth the May-day's jocund sun;
So through his inlaced wrinkles broke
A nature bright, a beaming one.

"Hidalgos, pardon! Strolling here
These fine old villa-sites to see,
I caught that good word penalty,
And could not otherwise than cheer.
Pray now, here be two, four, six, eight—
Ten legs; I'll add one more, by leave,
And eke an arm."
In hobbling state
He came among them, with one sleeve
Loose flying, and one wooden limb,
A leg. All eyes the cripple skim;
Each rises, and his seat would give:
But Derwent in advance: "Why, Don—
My good Don Hannibal, I mean;
Senor Don Hannibal Rohon
Del Aquaviva—a good e'en!"
"Ha, thou, is't thou?" the other cried,
And peered and stared not unamazed;
Then flung his one arm round him wide:
Then at arm's length: "St. James be praised,
With all the calendar!"
"But, tell:
What wind wafts here Don Hannibal?
When last I left thee at 'The Cock'
In Fleet Street, thou wert like a rock
For England—bent on anchoring there."
"Oh, too much agitation; yes,
Too proletarian it proved.
I've stumped about since; no redress;
Norway's too cold; Egypt's all glare;
And everywhere that I removed

This cursed Progress still would greet.
Ah where (thought I) in Old World view
Some blest asylum from the New!
At last I steamed for Joppa's seat,
Resolved on Asia for retreat.
Asia for me, Asia will do.
But just where to pitch tent—invest—

Ah, that's the point; I'm still in quest,
Don Derwent.—Look, the sun falls low;
But lower the funds in Mexico
Whereto he's sinking."
"Gentlemen:"
Said Derwent, turning on them then;
"I introduce and do commend
To ye Don Hannibal Rohon;
He is my estimable friend
And well beloved. Great fame he's won
In war. Those limbs—"
"St. James defend!"
Here cried Don Hannibal; "stop! stop!
Pulled down is Montezuma's hall!—
Hidalgos, I am, as ye see,
Just a poor cripple—that is all;
A cripple, yet contrive to hop
Far off from Mexic liberty,
Thank God! I lost these limbs for that;
And would that they were mine again,
And all were back to former state—
I, Mexico, and poor Old Spain.
And for Don Derwent here, my friend—
You know his way. And so I end,
Poor penitent American:
Oh, 'tis the sorriest thing! In me
A reformado reformed ye see.

Ungar, a very Indian here
Too serious far to take a jest,
Or rather, who no sense possessed
Of humor; he, for aye austere,
Took much in earnest; and a light
Of attestation over-bright
Shot from his eyes, though part suppressed.
"But penalties, these penalties, "
Here cried the crippled one again;
"Proceed, hidalgo; name you these
Same capital good penalties:
They're needed."
"Hold, let me explain,"
Cried Derwent: "We, as meek as worms—
Oh, far from taking any pique
As if the kind but formed a clique—
Have late been hearing in round terms
The sore disparagement of man,
Don Hannibal." "You think I'll ban?
Disparage him with all my heart!

What villain takes the rascal's part?
Advance the argument."
"But stay:
'Tis too much odds now; it won't do,
Such reinforcement come. Nay, nay,
I of the Old World, all alone
Maintaining hope and ground for cheer
'Gainst ye, the offspring of the New?
Ah, what reverses time can own!"
So Derwent light. But earnest here,
Ungar: "Old World? if age's test
Be this—advanced experience,
Then, in the truer moral sense,
Ours is the Old World. You, at best,
In dreams of your advanced Reform,
Adopt the cast skin of our worm."
"Hey, hey!" exclaimed Don Hannibal;
"Not cast yet quite; the snake is sick—
Would wriggle out. 'Tis pitiful!
But brave times for the empiric.—
You spake now of Reform. For me,
Among reformers in true way
There's one—the imp of Semele;
Ay, and brave Raleigh too, we'll say.
Wine and the weed! blest innovations,
How welcome to the weary nations!
But what's in this Democracy?
Eternal hacking! Woe is me,
She lopped these limbs, Democracy."
"Ah, now, Don Hannibal Rohon
Del Aquaviva!" Derwent cried;
"I knew it: two upon a side!"
But Ungar, earnest in his plea—
Intent, nor caring to have done;
And turning where suggestion led
At tangent: "Ay, Democracy
Lops, lops; but where's her planted bed?
The future, what is that to her
Who vaunts she's no inheritor?
'Tis in her mouth, not in her heart.
The Past she spurns, though 'tis the past
From which she gets her saving part—
That Good which lets her Evil last.
Behold her whom the panders crown,
Harlot on horseback, riding down
The very Ephesians who acclaim
This great Diana of ill fame!
Arch strumpet of an impious age,

Upstart from ranker villanage,
'Tis well she must restriction taste
Nor lay the world's broad manor waste:
Asia shall stop her at the least,
That old inertness of the East.
She's limited; lacking the free
And genial catholicity
Which in Christ's pristine scheme unfurled
Grace to the city and the world."
"By Cotopaxi, a brave vent!"
(And here he took a pinch of snuff,
Flapping the spill off with loose cuff)
"Good, excellenza—excellent!
But, pardon me," in altered tone;
"I'm sorry, but I must away;"
And, setting crutch, he footing won;
"We're just arrived in cloister there,
Our little party; and they stay
My coming for the convent-fare.
Adieu: we'll meet anon—we'll meet,
Don Derwent. Nay, now, never stir;
Not I would such a group unseat;
But happy the good rein and spur
That brought thee where once more we greet.
Good e'en, Don Derwent—not good-by;
And, cavaliers, the evil eye
Keep far from ye!" He limped away,
Rolling a wild ranchero lay:
"House your cattle and stall your steed:
Stand by, stand by for the great stampede!"

Canto XX - Derwent and Ungar

"Not thou com'st in the still small voice,"
Said Derwent, "thou queer Mexican!"
And followed him with eyes: "This man,"
And turned here, "he likes not grave talk,
The settled undiluted tone;
It does his humorous nature balk.

'Twas ever too his sly rebuff,
While yet obstreperous in praise,
Taking that dusty pinch of snuff.
An oddity, he has his ways;
Yet trust not, friends, the half he says:
Not he would do a weasel harm;

A secret agent of Reform;
At least, that is my theory."
"The quicksilver is quick to skim,"
Ungar remarked, with eye on him.
"Yes, nature has her levity,"
Dropped Derwent.
Nothing might disarm
The other; he: "Your word reform:
What meaning's to that word assigned?
From Luther's great initial down,
Through all the series following on
The impetus augments—the blind
Precipitation: blind, for tell
Whitherward does the surge impel?
The end, the aim? 'Tis mystery."
"Oh, no. Through all methinks I see
The object clear: belief revised,
Men liberated—equalized
In happiness. No mystery,
Just none at all; plain sailing."
"Well,
Assume this: is it feasible?
Your methods? These are of the world:
Now the world cannot save the world;
And Christ renounces it. His faith,
Breaking with every mundane path,
Aims straight at heaven. To founded thrones
He says: Trust not to earthly stanchions
And unto poor and houseless ones—
My Father's house has many mansions.
Warning and solace be but this;
No thought to mend a world amiss."
"Ah now, ah now!" plead Derwent.
"Nay,
Test further; take another way:
Go ask Aurelius Antonine—
A Caesar wise, grave, just, benign,
Lord of the world—why, in the calm
Which through his reign the empire graced—
Why he, that most considerate heart
Superior, and at vantage placed,
Contrived no secular reform,
Though other he knew not, nor balm."
"Alas," cried Derwent (and, in part,
As vainly longing for retreat)
"Though good Aurelius was a man
Matchless in mind as sole in seat,
Yet pined he under numbing ban

Of virtue without Christian heat:
As much you intimated too,
Just saying that no balm he knew.
Howbeit, true reform goes on
By Nature; doing, never done.
Mark the advance: creeds drop the hate;
Events still liberalize the state."
"But tell: do men now more cohere
In bonds of duty which sustain?
Cliffs crumble, and the parts regain
A liberal freedom, it is clear.
And for conventicles—I fear,
Much as a hard heart aged grown
Abates in rigor, losing tone;
So sects decrepit, at death's door,
Dote into peace through loss of power."
"You put it so," said Derwent light:
"No more developments to cite?"
"Ay, quench the true, the mock sun fails
Therewith. Much so, Hypocrisy,
The false thing, wanes just in degree
That Faith, the true thing, wanes: each pales.
There's one development; 'tis seen
In masters whom not low ye rate:
What lack, in some outgivings late,
Of the old Christian style toward men—
I do not mean the wicked ones,
But Pauperism's unhappy sons
In cloud so blackly ominous,
Grimy in Mammon's English pen—
Collaterals of his overplus:
How worse than them Immanuel fed
On hill-top—helped and comforted.
Thou, Poverty, erst free from shame,
Even sacred through the Savior's claim,
Professed by saints, by sages prized—
A pariah now, and bastardized!

Reactions from the Christian plan
Bear others further. Quite they shun
A god to name, or cite a man
Save Greek, heroical, a Don:
'Tis Plato's aristocratic tone.
All recognition they forego
Of Evil; supercilious skim
With spurious wing of seraphim
The last abyss. Freemen avow
Belief in right divine of Might,

Yet spurn at kings. This is the light—
Divine the darkness. Mark the way
The Revolution, whose first mode
Ere yet the maniacs overrode,
Despite the passion of the dream
Evinced no disrespect for God;
Mark how, in our denuding day,
E'en with the masses, as would seem
It tears the fig-leaf quite away.
Contrast these incidents: The mob,
The Paris mob of Eighty-nine,
Haggard and bleeding, with a throb
Burst the long Tuileries. In shrine
Of chapel there, they saw the Cross
And Him thereon. Ah, bleeding Man,
The people's friend, thou bled'st for us
Who here bleed, too! Ragged they ran—
They took the crucifix; in van
They put it, marched with drum and psalm
And throned it in their Notre Dame.
But yesterday—how did they then,
In new uprising of the Red,
The offspring of those Tuileries men?
They made a clothes-stand of the Cross
Before the church; and, on that head
Which bowed for them, could wanton toss
The sword-belt, while the gibing sped.
Transeended rebel angels! Woe
To us; without a God, 'tis woe!"

Canto XXI - Ungar and Rolfe

"Such earnestness! such wear and tear,
And man but a thin gossamer!"
So here the priest aside; then turned,
And, starting: "List! the vesper-bell?
Nay, nay—the hour is passed. But, oh,
He must have supped, Don Hannibal,
Ere now. Come, friends, and shall we go?
This hot discussion, let it stand
And cool; to-morrow we'll remand."
"Not yet, I pray," said Rolfe; "a word;"
And turned toward Ungar; "be adjured,
And tell us if for earth may be
In ripening arts, no guarantee
Of happy sequel."

"Arts are tools;
But tools, they say are to the strong:
Is Satan weak? weak is the Wrong?
No blessed augury overrules:
Your arts advance in faith's decay:
You are but drilling the new Hun
Whose growl even now can some dismay;
Vindictive in his heart of hearts,
He schools him in your mines and marts—
A skilled destroyer."

"But, need own
That portent does in no degree
Westward impend, across the sea."
"Over there? And do ye not forebode?
Against pretenses void or weak
The impieties of 'Progress' speak.
What say these, in effect, to God?
'How profits it? And who art Thou
That we should serve Thee? Of Thy ways
No knowledge we desire; new ways
We have found out, and better. Go—
Depart from us; we do erase
Thy sinecure: behold, the sun
Stands still no more in Ajalon:
Depart from us!'—And if He do?
(And that He may, the Scripture says)
Is aught betwixt ye and the hells?
For He, nor in irreverent view,
'Tis He distills that savor true
Which keeps good essences from taint;
Where He is not, corruption dwells,
And man and chaos are without restraint."
"Oh, oh, you do but generalize
In void abstractions."
"Hypothesize:
If be a people which began
Without impediment, or let
From any ruling which fore-ran;
Even striving all things to forget
But this—the excellence of man
Left to himself, his natural bent,
His own devices and intent;
And if, in satire of the heaven,
A world, a new world have been given
For stage whereon to deploy the event;
If such a people be—well, well,
One hears the kettle-drums of hell!

Exemplary act awaits its place
In drama of the human race."
"Is such act certain?" Rolfe here ran
"Not much is certain."
"God is—man.
The human nature, the divine—
Have both been proved by many a sign.
'Tis no astrologer and star.
The world has now so old become,
Historic memory goes so far
Backward through long defiles of doom;
Whoso consults it honestly
That mind grows prescient in degree
For man, like God abides the same
Always, through ail variety
Of woven garments to the frame."
"Yes, God is God, and men are men,
Forever and for aye. What then?
There's Circumstance there's Time; and these
Are charged with store of latencies
Still working in to modify.
For mystic text that you recall,
Dilate upon, and e'en apply—
(Although I seek not to decry)
Theology's scarce practical.
But leave this: the New World's the theme.
Here, to oppose your dark extreme,
(Since an old friend is good at need)
To an old thought I'll fly. Pray, heed:
Those waste-weirs which the New World yields
To inland freshets—the free vents
Supplied to turbid elements;
The vast reserves—the untried fields;
These long shall keep off and delay
The class-war, rich-and-poor-man fray
Of history. From that alone
Can serious trouble spring. Even that
Itself, this good result may own—
The first firm founding of the state."
Here ending, with a watchful air
Inquisitive, Rolfe waited him.

And Ungar:
"True heart do ye bear
In this discussion? or but trim
To draw my monomania out,
For monomania, past doubt,
Some of ye deem it. Yet I'll on.

Yours seems a reasonable tone;
But in the New World things make haste:
Not only men, the state lives fast—
Fast breeds the pregnant eggs and shells,
The slumberous combustibles
Sure to explode. 'Twill come, 'twill come!
One demagogue can trouble much:
How of a hundred thousand such?
And universal suffrage lent
To back them with brute element
Overwhelming? What shall bind these seas
Of rival sharp communities
Unchristianized? Yea, but 'twill come!"
"What come?"
"Your Thirty Years (of) War."
"Should fortune's favorable star
Avert it?"
"Fortune? nay, 'tis doom."
"Then what comes after? spasms but tend
Ever, at last, to quiet."
"Know,
Whatever happen in the end,
Be sure 'twill yield to one and all
New confirmation of the fall
Of Adam. Sequel may ensue,
Indeed, whose germs one now may view:
Myriads playing pygmy parts—
Debased into equality:
In glut of all material arts
A civic barbarism may be:
Man disennobled—brutalized
By popular science—Atheized
Into a smatterer "
"Oh, oh!"
"Yet knowing all self need to know
In self's base little fallacy;
Dead level of rank commonplace:
An Anglo-Saxon China, see,
May on your vast plains shame the race
In the Dark Ages of Democracy."

America!
In stilled estate,
On him, half-brother and co-mate—
In silence, and with vision dim
Rolfe, Vine, and Clarel gazed on him;
They gazed, nor one of them found heart
To upbraid the crotchet of his smart,

Bethinking them whence sole it came,
Though birthright he renounced in hope,
Their sanguine country's wonted claim.
Nor dull they were in honest tone
To some misgivings of their own:
They felt how far beyond the scope
Of elder Europe's saddest thought
Might be the New World's sudden brought
In youth to share old age's pains—
To feel the arrest of hope's advance,
And squandered last inheritance;
And cry—"To Terminus build fanes!
Columbus ended earth's romance:
No New World to mankind remains!"

Canto XXII - Of Wickedness the Word

Since, for the charity they knew,
None cared the exile to upbraid
Or further breast—while yet he threw,
In silence that oppressive weighed,
The after-influence of his spell—
The priest in light disclaimer said
To Rolfe apart: "The icicle,
The dagger-icicle draws blood;
But give it sun!" "You mean his mood
Is accident—would melt away
In fortune's favorable ray.
But if 'tis happiness he lacks,
Why, let the gods warm all cold backs
With that good sun. But list!"
In vent
Of thought, abrupt the malcontent:
"What incantation shall make less
The ever-upbubbling wickedness!
Is this fount nature's?"
Under guard
Asked Vine: "Is wickedness the word?"
"The right word? Yes; but scarce the thing
Is there conveyed; for one need know
Wicked has been the tampering
With wickedness the word " "Even so?"
"Ay, ridicule's light sacrilege
Has taken off the honest edge—
Quite turned aside—perverted all
That Saxon term and Scriptural."

"Restored to the incisive wedge,
What means it then, this wickedness?
Ungar regarded him with look
Of steady search: "And wilt thou brook?
Thee leaves it whole.?—This wickedness
(Might it retake true import well)
Means not default, nor vulgar vice,
Nor Adam's lapse in Paradise;
But worse: 'twas this evoked the hell—
Gave in the conscious soul's recess
Credence to Calvin. What's implied
In that deep utterance decried
Which Christians labially confess—
Be born anew?"
"Ah, overstate
Thou dost!" the priest sighed; "but look there!
No jarring theme may violate
Yon tender evening sky! How fair
These olive-orchards: see, the sheep
Mild drift toward the folds of sleep.
The blessed Nature! still her glance
Returns the love she well receives
From hearts that with the stars advance,
Each heart that in the goal believes!"
Ungar, though nettled, as might be,
At these bland substitutes in plea
(By him accounted so) yet sealed
His lips. In fine, all seemed to yield
With one consent a truce to talk.

But Clarel, who, since that one hour
Of unreserve on Saba's tower,
Less relished Derwent's pleasant walk
Of myrtles, hardly might remain
Uninfluenced by Ungar's vein:
If man in truth be what you say,
And such the prospects for the clay,
And outlook of the future cease!
What's left us but the senses' sway?
Sinner, sin out life's petty lease:
We are not worth the saving. Nay,
For me, if thou speak true but ah,
Yet, yet there gleams one beckoning star—
So near the horizon, judge I right
That 'tis of heaven?
But wanes the light—
The evening Angelus is rolled:
They rise, and seek the convent's fold.

Canto XXIII - Derwent and Rolfe

There as they wend, Derwent his arm,
Demure, and brotherly, and grave,
Slips into Rolfe's: "A bond we have;
We lock, we symbolize it, see;

Yes, you and I: but he, but he!"
And checked himself, as under warm
Emotion. Rolfe kept still. "Unlike,
Unlike! Don Hannibal through storm
Has passed; yet does his sunshine strike.
But Ungar, clouded man! No balm
He'll find in that unhappy vein;"
Pausing, awaiting Rolfe again.
Rolfe held his peace. "But grant indeed
His strictures just—how few will heed!
The hippopotamus is tough;
Well bucklered too behind. Enough:
Man has two sides: keep on the bright."

"Two sides imply that one's not right;
So that won't do."—"Wit, wit!"—"Nay, truth."
"Sententious are ye, pithy—sooth!"
Yet quickened now that Rolfe began
To find a tongue, he sprightlier ran:
"As for his Jeremiad spells,
Shall these the large hope countermand?
The world's outlived the oracles,
And the people never will disband!
Stroll by my hedge-rows in the June,
The chirruping quite spoils his tune."
"Ay, birds," said Rolfe; nor more would own.
"But, look: to hold the censor-tone,
One need be qualified: is he?"
"He's wise." "Too vehemently wise!
His factious memories tyrannize
And wrest the judgment." "In degree,
Perchance." "But come: shall we accord
Credentials to that homely sword
He wears? Would it had more of grace!
But 'tis in serviceable case."
"Right! war's his business." "Business, say you?"
Resenting the unhandsome word;
"Unsay it quickly, friend, I pray you!

Fine business driving men through fires
To Hades, at the bidding blind
Of Heaven knows whom! but, now I mind,
In this case 'tis the Turk that hires
A Christian for that end."—"May be,"
Said Rolfe. "And pretty business too
Is war for one who did instill
So much concern for Lincoln Hugh
Ground up by Mammon in the mill.
Or was it rhetoric?" "May be,"
Said Rolfe. "And let me hint, may be
You're curt to-day. But, yes, I see:
Your countryman he is. Well, well,
That's right—you're right; no more I'll dwell:
Your countryman; and, yes, at heart
Rather you sidled toward his part
Though playing well the foil, pardee!
Oh, now you stare: no need: a trick
To deal your dullish mood a prick.
But mind you, though, some things you said
By Jordan lounging in the shade
When our discourse so freely ran?
But whatsoe'er reserves be yours
Touching your native clime and clan,
And whatsoe'er his thought abjures;
Still, when he's criticised by one
Not of the tribe, not of the zone
Chivalric still, though doggedly,
You stand up for a countryman:
I like your magnanimity;"
And silent pressed the enfolded arm
As he would so transmit a charm
Along the nerve, which might insure,
However cynic challenge ran,
Faith genial in at least one man
Fraternal in love's overture.

Canto XXIV – Twilight

"Over the river
In gloaming, ah, still do ye plain?
Dove dove in the mangroves,
How dear is thy pain!

"Sorrow—but fondled;
Reproaches that never upbraid

Spite the passion, the yearning
Of love unrepaid.

"Teach me, oh! teach me
Thy cadence, that Inez may thrill
With the bliss of the sadness,
And love have his will!"

Through twilight of mild evening pale,
As now returning slow they fare
In dubious keeping with the dale
And legends, floating came that air
From one invisible in shade,
Singing and lightly sauntering on
Toward the cloisters. Pause they made;
But he a lateral way had won:
Viewless he passed, as might a wave
Rippling, which doth a frigate lave
At anchor in the midnight road.

Clarel a fleeting thought bestowed:
Unkenned! to thee what thoughts belong—
Announced by such a tropic song.

Canto XXV - The Invitation

Returned to harbor, Derwent sought
His Mexic friend; and him he found
At home in by-place of a court
Of private kind—some tools around,
And planks and joiner's stuff, and more,
With little things, and odds and ends,
Conveniences which ease commends
Unto some plain old bachelor.
And here, indeed, one such a stay
At whiles did make; a placid friar,
A sexton gratis in his way,
When some poor brother did require
The last fraternal offices.
This funeral monk, now much at ease,
Uncowled, upon a work-bench sat—
Lit by a greenish earthen lamp
(With cross-bones baked thereon for stamp)
Behind him placed upon a mat—
Engaged in gossip, old men's chat,
With the limb-lopped Eld of Mexico;

Who, better to sustain him so
On his one leg, had niched him all
In one of some strange coffins there,
A 'lean and open by the wall
Like sentry-boxes.—
"Take a chair,
Don Derwent; no, I mean—yes, take
A—coffin; come, be sociable."
"Don Hannibal, Don Hannibal,
What see I? Well, for pity's sake!"
"Eh? This is brother Placido,
And we are talking of old times,
For, learn thou, that in Mexico
First knew he matins and the chimes.
But, come, get in; there's nothing else;
'Tis easy; here one lazy dwells
Almost as in a barber's chair;
See now, I lean my head."
"Ah, yes;
But I—don't—feel the weariness:
Thanks, thanks; no, I the bench prefer.—
Good brother Placido, I'm glad
You find a countryman." And so
For little time discourse he made;
But presently—the monk away
Being called—proposed that they should go,
He and Don Hannibal the gray,
And in refectory sit down
That talk might more convenient run.
The others through the courts diverge,
Till all to cots conducted fare
Where reveries in slumber merge,
While lulling steals from many a cell
A bee-like buzz of bed-side prayer—
Night in the hive monastical.

And now—not wantonly designed
Like lays in grove of Daphne sung,
But helping to fulfill the piece
Which in these cantoes finds release,
Appealing to the museful mind—
A chord, the satyr's chord is strung.

Canto XXVI - The Prodigal

In adolescence thrilled by hope

Which fain would verify the gleam
And find if destiny concur,
How dwells upon life's horoscope
Youth, always an astrologer,
Forecasting happiness the dream!

Slumber interred them; but not all,
For so it chanced that Clarel's cell
Was shared by one who did repel
The poppy. 'Twas a prodigal,
Yet pilgrim too in casual way,
And seen within the grots that day,
But only seen, no more than that.
In years he might be Clarel's mate.
Not talkative, he half reclined
In revery of dreamful kind;
Or might the fable, the romance
Be tempered by experience?
For ruling under spell serene,
A light precocity is seen.
That mobile face, voluptuous air
No Northern origin declare,
But Southern—where the nations bright,
The costumed nations, circled be
In garland round a tideless sea
Eternal in its fresh delight.
Nor less he owned the common day;
His avocation naught, in sooth—
A toy of Mammon; but the ray
And fair aureola of youth
Deific makes the prosiest clay.
From revery now by Clarel won
He brief his story entered on:
A native of the banks of Rhone
He traveled for a Lyons house
Which dealt in bales luxurious;
Detained by chance at Jaffa gray,
Rather than let ripe hours decay,
He'd run o'er, in a freak of fun,
Green Sharon to Jerusalem,
And thence, not far, to Bethlehem.
Thy silvery voice, irreverent one!
'Twas musical; and Clarel said:
"Greatly I err, or thou art he
Who singing along the hill-side sped
At fall of night."
"And heard you me?
'Twas sentimental, to be sure:

A little Spanish overture,
A Tombez air, which months ago
A young Peruvian let flow.
Locked friends we were; he's gone home now."
To Clarel 'twas a novel style
And novel nature; and awhile
Mutely he dwelt upon him here.
Earnest to know how the most drear
Solemnity of Judah's glade
Affect might such a mind, he said
Something to purpose; but he shied.
One essay more; whereat he cried:
"Amigo! favored lads there are,
Born under such a lucky star,
They weigh not things too curious, see,
Albeit conforming to their time
And usages thereof, and clime:
Well, mine's that happy family."
The student faltered—felt annoy:
Absorbed in problems ill-defined,
Am I too curious in my mind;
And, baffled in the vain employ,
Foregoing many an easy joy?
That thought he hurried from; and so
Unmindful in perturbed estate
Of that light intimation late,
He said: "On hills of dead Judaoa
Wherever one may faring go,
He dreams—Fit place to set the bier
Of Jacob, brought from Egypt's mead:
Here's Atad's threshing-floor."
"Indeed? "
Scarce audible was that in tone;
Nor Clarel heard it, but went on:
"'Tis Jephthah's daughter holds the hight;
She, she's the muse here.—But, I pray,
Confess to Judah's mournful sway."
He held his peace. "You grant the blight?"
"No Boulevards." "Do other lands
Show equal ravage you've beheld?"
"Oh, yes," and eyed his emerald
In ring. "But here a God commands,
A judgment dooms: you that gainsay?"
Up looked he quick, then turned away,
And with a shrug that gave mute sign
That here the theme he would decline.
But Clarel urged. As in despair
The other turned—invoked the air:

"Was it in such talk, Don Rovenna,
We dealt in Seville, I and you?
No! chat of love-wile and duenna
And saya-manto in Peru.
Ah, good Limeno, dear amigo,
What times were ours, the holidays flew;
Life, life a revel and clear allegro;
But home thou'rt gone; pity, but true!"
At burst so lyrical, yet given
Not all without some mock in leaven,
Once more did Clarel puzzled sit;
But rallying in spite of it,
Continued: "Surely now, 'tis clear
That in the aspect of Judaea—"
"My friend, it is just naught to me!
Why, why so pertinacious be?
Refrain!" Here, turning light away,
As quitting so the theme: "How gay
Damascus! orchard of a town:
Not yet she's heard the tidings though."
"Tidings?"
"Tidings of long ago:
Isaiah's dark burden, malison:
Of course, to be perpetual fate:
Bat, serpent, screech-owl, and all that.
But truth is, grace and pleasure there,
In Abana and Pharpar's streams
(O shady haunts! O sherbert-air!)
So twine the place in odorous dreams,
How may she think to mope and moan,
The news not yet being got to town
That she's a ruin! Oh, 'tis pity,
For she, she is earth's senior city!—
Pray, who was he, that man of state
Whose footman at Elisha's gate
Loud rapped? The name has slipped. Howe'er,
That Damascene maintained it well:
'We've better streams than Israel,
Yea, fairer waters.' "Weetless here
Clarel betrayed half cleric tone:
"Naaman, you mean. Poor leper one,
'Twas Jordan healed him. "
"As you please."
And hereupon the Lyonese—
(Capricious, or inferring late
That he had yielded up his state
To priggish inroad) gave mute sign
'Twere well to end.

"But Palestine,
Insisted Clarel, "do you not
Concede some strangeness to her lot?"

"Amigo, how you persecute!
You all but tempt one to refute
These stale megrims. You of the West,
What devil has your hearts possessed,
You can't enjoy?—Ah, dear Rovenna,
With talk of donna and duenna,
You came too from that hemisphere,
But freighted with quite other cheer:
No pedant, no!" Then, changing free,
Laughed with a light audacity:
"Well, me for one, dame Judah here
Don't much depress: she's not austere—
Nature has lodged her in good zone—
The true wine-zone of Noah: the Cape
Yields no such bounty of the grape.
Hence took King Herod festal tone;
Else why the tavern-cluster gilt
Hang out before that fane he built
The second temple?" Catching thus
A buoyant frolic impetus,
He bowled along: "Herewith agrees
The ducat of the Maccabees,
Graved with the vine. Methinks I see
The spies from Eshcol, full of glee
Trip back to camp with clusters swung
From jolting pole on shoulders hung:
'Cheer up, 'twill do; it needs befit;
Lo ye, behold the fruit of it!'
And, tell me, does not Solomon's harp
(Oh, that it should have taken warp
In end!) confirm the festa? Hear:
'Thy white neck is like ivory;
I feed among thy lilies, dear:
Stay me with flagons, comfort me
With apples; thee would I enclose!
Thy twin breasts are as two young roes.' "

Clarel protested, yet as one
Part lamed in candor; and took tone
In formal wise: "Nay, pardon me,
But you misdeem it: Solomon's Song
Is allegoric—needs must be."
"Proof, proof, pray, if 'tis not too long."
"Why, Saint Bernard "

"Who? Sir Bernard?
Never that knight for me left card!"
"No, Saint Bernard, 'twas he of old
The Song's hid import first unrolled—
Confirmed in every after age:
The chapter-headings on the page
Of modern Bibles (in that Song)
Attest his rendering, and prolong:
A mystic burden."
"Eh? so too
The Bonzes Hafiz' rhyme construe
Which lauds the grape of Shiraz. See,
They cant that in his frolic fire
Some bed-rid fakir would aspire
In foggy symbols. Me, oh me!—
What stuff of Levite and Divine!
Come, look at straight things more in line,
Blue eyes or black, which like you best?
Your Bella Donna, how's she dressed?"
'Twas very plain this sprightly youth
Little suspected the grave truth
That he, with whom he thus made free,
A student was, a student late
Of reverend theology:
Nor Clarel was displeased thereat.
The other now: "There is no tress
Can thrall one like a Jewess's.
A Hebrew husband, Hebrew-wed,
Is wondrous faithful, it is said;
Which needs be true; for, I suppose,
As bees are loyal to the rose,
So men to beauty. Of his girls,
On which did the brown Indian king,
Ahasuerus, shower his pearls?

Why, Esther: Judah wore the ring.
And Nero, captain of the world,
His arm about a Jewess curled—
Bright spouse, Poppaea. And with good will
Some Christian monarchs share the thrill,
In palace kneeling low before
Crowned Judah, like those nobs of yore.
These Hebrew witches! well-a-day
Of Jeremiah what reck they?"

Clarel looked down: was he depressed?
The prodigal resumed: "Earth's best,
Earth's loveliest portrait, daintiest

Reveals Judaean grace and form:
Urbino's ducal mistress fair—
Ay, Titian's Venus, golden-warm.
Her lineage languishes in air
Mysterious as the unfathomed sea:
That grave, deep Hebrew coquetry!
Thereby Bathsheba David won
In bath a purposed bait!—Have done!—
Blushing? The cuticle's but thin!
Blushing? yet you my mind would win.
Priests make a goblin of the Jew:
Shares he not flesh with me—with you?"
What wind was this? And yet it swayed
Even Clarel's cypress. He delayed
All comment, gazing at him there.
Then first he marked the clustering hair
Which on the bright and shapely brow
At middle part grew slantly low:
Rich, tumbled, chestnut hood of curls
Like to a Polynesian girl's,
Who, inland eloping with her lover,
The deacon-magistrates recover—
With sermon and black bread reprove
Who fed on berries and on love.
So young (thought Clarel) yet so knowing;
With much of dubious at the heart,
Yet winsome in the outward showing;
With whom, with what, hast thou thy part?
In flaw upon the student's dream
A wafture of suspicion stirred:
He spake: "The Hebrew, it would seem,
You study much; you have averred
More than most Gentiles well may glean
In voyaging mere from scene to scene
Of shifting traffic." Irksomeness
Here vexed the other's light address;
But, ease assuming, gay he said:
"Oh, in my wanderings, why, I've met,
Among all kinds, Hebrews well-read,
And some nor dull nor bigot-bred;
Yes, I pick up, nor all forget."
So saying, and as to be rid
Of further prosing, he undid
His vesture, turned him, smoothed his cot:
"Late, late; needs sleep, though sleep's a sot."
"A word," cried Clarel: "bear with me:
Just nothing strange at all you see
Touching the Hebrews and their lot?"

Recumbent here: "Why, yes, they share
That oddity the Gypsies heir:
About them why not make ado?
The Parsees are an odd tribe too;
Dispersed, no country, and yet hold
By immemorial rites, we're told.
Amigo, do not scourge me on;
Put up, put up your monkish thong!
Pray, pardon now; by peep of sun
Take horse I must. Good night, with song:
"Lights of Shushan, if your urn
Mellow shed the opal ray,
To delude one—damsels, turn,
Wherefore tarry? why betray?

Drop your garlands and away!
Leave me, phantoms that but feign;
Sting me not with inklings vain!

"But, if magic none prevail,
Mocking in untrue romance;
Let your Paradise exhale
Odors; and enlink the dance;
And, ye rosy feet, advance
Till ye meet morn's ruddy Hours
Unabashed in Shushan's bowers!"

No more: they slept. A spell came down
And Clarel dreamed, and seemed to stand
Betwixt a Shushan and a sand
The Lyonese was lord of one,
The desert did the Tuscan own,
The pale pure monk. A zephyr fanned;
It vanished, and he felt the strain
Of clasping arms which would detain
His heart from such ascetic range.
He woke; 'twas day; he was alone,
The Lyonese being up and gone:
Vital he knew organic change,
Or felt, at least, that change was working—
A subtle innovator lurking.
He rose, arrayed himself, and won
The roof to take the dawn's fresh air,
And heard a ditty, and looked down.
Who singing rode so debonair?
His cell-mate, flexible young blade,
Mounted in rear of cavalcade
Just from the gate, in rythmic way

Switching a light malacca gay:
"Rules, who rules?
Fools the wise, makes wise the fools—
Every ruling overrules?
Who the dame that keeps the house,
Provides the diet, and oh, so quiet,
Brings all to pass, the slyest mouse?
Tell, tell it me:
Signora Nature, who but she!"

Canto XXVII - By Parapet

"Well may ye gaze! What's good to see
Better than Adam's humanity
When genial lodged! Such spell is given,
It lured the staid grandees of heaven,
Though biased in their souls divine
Much to one side the feminine.—
He is the pleasantest small fellow!"

It was the early-rising priest,
Who up there in the morning mellow
Had followed Clarel: "Not the least
Of pleasures here which I have known
Is meeting with that laxer one.
We talked below; but all the while
My thoughts were wandering away,
Though never once mine eyes did stray,
He did so pleasingly beguile
To keep them fixed upon his form:
Such harmony pervades his warm
Soft outline.—Why now, what a stare
Of incredulity you speak
From eyes! But it was some such fair
Young sinner in the time antique
Suggested to the happy Greek
His form of Bacchus—the sweet shape!
Young Bacchus, mind ye, not the old:
The Egyptian ere he crushed the grape.—
But—how? and home-sick are you? Come,
What's in your thoughts, pray? Wherefore mum?
So Derwent; though but ill he sped,
Clarel declining to be led
Or cheered. Nor less in covert way
That talk might have an after-sway
Beyond the revery which ran

Half-heeded now or dim: This man—
May Christian true such temper wish?
His happiness seems paganish.

Canto XXVIII - David's Well

The Lyonese had joined a train
Whereof the man of scars was one
Whose office led him further on
And barring longer stay. Farewell
He overnight had said, ere cell
He sought for slumber. Brief the word;
No hand he grasped; yet was he stirred,
Despite his will, in heart at core:
'Twas countrymen he here forsook:
He felt it; and his aspect wore
In the last parting, that strange look
Of one enlisted for sad fight
Upon some desperate dark shore,
Who bids adieu to the civilian,
Returning to his club-house bright,
In city cheerful with the million.
But Nature never heedeth this:
To Nature nothing is amiss.

It was a morning full of vent
And bustle. Other pilgrims went.
Later, accoutered in array
Don Hannibal and party sate
In saddle at the convent gate,
For Hebron bound.—"Ah, well-a-day!
I'm bolstered up here, tucked away:
My spare spar lashed behind, ye see;
This crutch for scepter. Come to me,
Embrace me my dear friend." and leant:
"I'm off for Mamre; under oak
Of Abraham I'll pitch my tent,
Perchance, far from the battle's smoke.
Good friars and friends, behold me here
A poor one-legged pioneer;
I go, I march, I am the man
In fore-front of the limping van
Of refluent emigration. So,
Farewell, Don Derwent; Placido,
Farewell; and God bless all and keep!—
Start, dragoman; come, take your sheep

To Hebron."
One among the rest
Attending the departure there
Was Clarel. Unto him, oppressed—
In travail of transition rare,
Scarce timely in its unconstraint
Was the droll Mexican's quirkish air
And humorous turn of hintings quaint.
The group dispersed.
Pleased by the hill
And vale, the minster, grot and vine,
Hardly the pilgrims found the will
To go and such fair scene decline.
But not less Bethlehem, avow,
Negative grew to him whose heart,
Swayed by love's nearer magnet now,
Would fain without delay depart;
Yet comradeship did still require
That some few hours need yet expire.
Restive, he sallied out alone,
And, ere long, place secluded won,
And there a well. The spot he eyed;
For fountains in that land, being rare,
Attention fix. "And, yes," he sighed,
Weighing the thing; "though everywhere
This vicinage quite altered be,
The well of Jesse's son I see;
For this in parched Adullam's lair
How sore he yearned: ah me, ah me,
That one would now upon me wait
With that sweet water by the gate!—
He stood: But who will bring to me
That living water which who drinks
He thirsteth not again! Let be:
A thirst that long may anguish thee,
Too long ungratified will die.
But whither now, my heart? wouldst fly
Each thing that keepeth not the pace
Of common uninquiring life?
What! fall back on clay commonplace?
Yearnest for peace so? sick of strife?
Yet how content thee with routine
Worldly? how mix with tempers keen
And narrow like the knife? how live
At all, if once a fugitive
From thy own nobler part, though pain
Be portion inwrought with the grain?"

But here, in fair accosting word,
A stranger's happy hail he heard
Descending from a vineyard nigh.
He turned: a pilgrim pleased his eye
(A Muscovite, late seen by shrine)
Good to behold—fresh as a pine—
Elastic, tall; complexion clear
As dawn in frosty atmosphere
Rose-tinged.
They greet. At once, to reach
Accord, the Russian said, "Sit here:
You sojourn with the Latin set,
I with the Greeks; but well we're met:
All's much the same: many waves, one beach.
I'm mateless now; one, and but one
I've taken to: and he's late gone.
You may have crossed him, for indeed
He tarried with your Latin breed
While here: a juicy little fellow—
A Seckel pear, so small and mellow."
"We shared a cell last night." "Ye did?
And, doubtless, into chat ye slid:
The theme, now; I am curious there."
"Judaea—the Jews. " With hightened air
The Russ rejoined: "And tell me, pray:
Who broached the topic? he?" "No, I;
And chary he in grudged reply
At first, but afterward gave way."
"Indeed?" the Russ, with meaning smile;
"But (further) did he aught revile?"
"The Jews, he said, were misconceived;
Much too he dropped which quite bereaved
The Scripture of its Runic spell.
But Runic said I? That's not well!
I alter, sure."
Not marking here
Clarel in his self-taxing cheer;
But full of his own thoughts in clew,
"Right, I was right!" the other cried:
"Evade he cannot, no, nor hide.
Learn, he who whiled the hour for you,
His race supplied the theme: a Jew!"
Clarel leaped up; "And can it be?
Some vague suspicion peered in me;
I sought to test it—test: and he—
Nay now, I mind me of a stir
Of color quick; and might it touch?"
And paused; then, as in slight demur:

"His cast of Hebrew is not much."
"Enough to badge him."
"Very well:
But why should he the badge repel?"
"Our Russian sheep still hate the mark;
They try to rub it off, nor cease
On hedge or briar to leave the fleece
In tell-tale tags. Well, much so he,
Averse to Aaron's cipher dark
And mystical. Society

Is not quite catholic, you know,
Retains some prejudices yet—
Likes not the singular; and so
He'd melt in, nor be separate—
Exclusive. And I see no blame.
Nor rare thing is it in French Jew,
Cast among strangers—traveling too—
To cut old grandsire Abraham
As out of mode. I talked, ere you
With this our friend. Let me avow
My late surmise is surety now."

They strolled, and parted. And amain
Confirmed the student felt the reign
Of reveries vague, which yet could mar,
Crossed by a surging element—
Surging while aiming at content:
So combs the billow ere it breaks upon the bar.

Canto XXIX - The Night Ride

It was the day preceding Lent,
Shrove Tuesday named in English old
(Forefathers' English), and content,
Some yet would tarry, to behold
The initiatory nocturn rite.
'Twas the small hour, as once again,
And final now, in mounted plight
They curve about the Bethlehem urn
Or vine-clad hollow of the swain,
And Clarel felt in every vein—
At last, Jerusalem! 'Twas thence
They started—thither they return,
Rounding the waste circumference.
Now Belex in his revery light

Rolls up and down those guineas bright
Whose minted recompense shall chink
In pouch of sash when travel's brink
Of end is won. Djalea in face
Wears an abstraction, lit by grace
Which governed hopes of rapture lend:
On coins his musings likewise bend—
The starry sequins woven fair
Into black tresses. But an air
Considerate and prudent reigns;
For his the love not vainly sure:
'Tis passion deep of man mature
For one who half a child remains:
Yes, underneath a look sedate,
What throbs are known!
But desolate
Upon the pilgrims strangely fall
Eclipses heavier far than come
To hinds, which, after carnival,
Return to toil and querulous home.
Revert did they? in mind recall
Their pilgrimage, yes, sum it all?
Could Siddim haunt them? Saba's bay?
Did the deep nature in them say—
Two, two are missing—laid away
In deserts twin? They let it be,
Nor spake; the candor of the heart
Shrank from suspected counterpart.
But one there was (and Clarel he)
Who, in his aspect free from cloud,
Here caught a gleam from source unspied,
As cliff may take on mountain-side,
When there one small brown cirque ye see,
Lit up in mole, how mellowly,
Day going down in somber shroud—
October-pall.
But tell the vein
Of new emotion, inly held,
That so the long contention quelled—
Languor, and indecision, pain.
Was it abrupt resolve? a strain
Wiser than wisdom's self might teach?

Yea, now his hand would boldly reach
And pluck the nodding fruit to him,
Fruit of the tree of life. If doubt
Spin spider-like her tissue out,
And make a snare in reason dim—

Why hang a fly in flimsy web?
One thing was clear, one thing in sooth:
Stays not the prime of June or youth:
At flood that tide makes haste to ebb.
Recurred one mute appeal of Ruth
(Now first aright construed, he thought),
She seemed to fear for him, and say:
"Ah, tread not, sweet, my father's way,
In whom this evil spirit wrought
And dragged us hither where we die!"
Yes, now would he forsake that road—
Alertly now and eager hie
To dame and daughter, where they trod
The Dolorosa—quick depart
With them and seek a happier sky.
Warblings he heard of hope in heart,
Responded to by duty's hymn;
He, late but weak, felt now each limb
In strength how buoyant. But, in truth,
Was part caprice, sally of youth?
What pulse was this with burning beat?
Whence, whence the passion that could give
Feathers to thought, yea, Mercury's feet?
The Lyonese, to sense so dear,
Nor less from faith a fugitive-
Had he infected Clarel here?
But came relapse: What end may prove?
Ah, almoner to Saba's dove,
Ah, bodeful text of hermit-rhyme!
But what! distrust the trustful eyes?
Are the sphered breasts full of mysteries
Which not the maiden's self may know?
May love's nice balance, finely slight,
Take tremor from fulfilled delight?

Can nature such a doom dispense
As, after ardor's tender glow,
To make the rapture more than pall
With evil secrets in the sense,
And guile whose bud is innocence
Sweet blossom of the flower of gall?
Nay, nay: Ah! God, keep far from me
Cursed Manes and the Manichee!
At large here life proclaims the law:
Unto embraces myriads draw
Through sacred impulse. Take thy wife;
Venture, and prove the soul of life,
And let fate drive.—So he the while,

In shadow from the ledges thrown,
As down the Bethlehem hill they file—
Abreast upon the plain anon
Advancing.
Far, in upland spot
A light is seen in Rama paling;
But Clarel sped, and heeded not,
At least recalled not Rachel wailing.

Aside they win a fountain clear,
The Cistern of the Kings—so named
Because (as vouched) the Magi here
Watered their camels, and reclaimed
The Ray, brief hid. Ere this they passed
Clarel looked in and there saw glassed
Down in the wave, one mellow star;
Then, glancing up, beheld afar
Enisled serene, the orb itself:—
Apt auspice here for journeying elf.

And now those skirting slopes they tread
Which devious bar the sunken bed
Of Hinnom. Thence uplifted shone
In hauntedness the deicide town
Faint silvered. Gates, of course, were barred;
But at the further eastern one,
St. Stephen's—there the turbaned guard
(To Belex known) at whispered word
Would ope. Thither, the nearer way,
By Jeremy's grot—they shun that ground,
For there an Ottoman camp's array
Deters. Through Hinnom now they push
Their course round Zion by the glen
Toward Rogel—whither shadowy rush
And where, at last, in cloud convene
(Ere, one, they sweep to gloomier hush)
Those two black chasms which enfold
Jehovah's hight. Flanking the well,
Ophel they turn, and gain the dell
Of Shaveh. Here the city old,
Fast locked in torpor, fixed in blight,
No hum sent forth, revealed no light:
Though, facing it, cliff-hung Siloam—
Sepulchral hamlet showed in tomb
A twinkling lamp. The valley slept—
Obscure, in monitory dream
Oppressive, roofed with awful skies
Whose stars like silver nail-heads gleam

Which stud some lid over lifeless eyes.

Canto XXX - The Valley of Decision

Delay!—Shall flute from forth the Gate
Issue, to warble welcome here—
Upon this safe returning wait
In gratulation? And, for cheer,
When inn they gain, there shall they see
The door-post wreathed?
Howe'er it be,
Through Clarel a revulsion ran,
Such as may seize debarking man
First hearing on Coquimbo's ground
That subterranean sullen sound
Which dull foreruns the shock. His heart,
In augury fair arrested here,
Upbraided him: Fool! and didst part
From Ruth? Strangely a novel fear
Obtruded—petty, and yet worse
And more from reason too averse,
Than that recurrent haunting bier
Molesting him erewhile. And yet
It was but irritation, fret—
Misgiving that the lines he writ
Upon the eve before the start
For Siddim, failed, or were unfit—
Came short of the occasion's tone:
To leave her, leave her in grief's smart:
To leave her—her, the stricken one:
Now first to feel full force of it!
Away! to be but there, but there!
Vain goadings: yet of love true part.
But then the pledge with letter sent,
Though but a trifle, still might bear
A token in dumb argument
Expressive more than words.
With knee
Straining against the saddle-brace,
He urges on; till, near the place
Of Hebrew graves, a light they see
Moving, and figures dimly trace:
Some furtive strange society.
Yet nearer as they ride, the light
Shuts down. "Abide!" enjoined the Druze;
"Waylayers these are none, but Jews,

Or I mistake, who here by night
Have stolen to do grave-digger's work.
During late outbreak in the town
The bigot in the baser Turk
Was so inflamed, some Hebrews dread
Assault, even here among their dead.
Abide a space; let me ride on."
Up pushed he, spake, allayed the fright
Of them who had shut down the light
At sound of comers.
Close they draw—
Advancing, lit by fan-shaped rays
Shot from a small dark-lantern's jaw
Presented pistol-like. They saw
Mattocks and men, in outline dim
On either ominous side of him
From whom went forth that point of blaze.
Resting from labor, each one stays
His implement on grave-stones old.
New-dug, between these, they behold
Two narrow pits: and (nor remote)
Twin figures on the ground they note
Folded in cloaks.
"And who rest there?
Rolfe sidelong asked.
"Our friends; have care!"
Replied the one that held in view
The lantern, slanting it a' shift,
Plainer disclosing them, and, too,
A broidered scarf, love's first chance gift,
The student's (which how well he knew!)
Binding one mantle's slender span.
With piercing cry, as one distraught,
Down from his horse leaped Clarel—ran
And hold of that cloak instant caught
And bared the face. Then (like a man
Shot through the heart, but who retains
His posture) rigid he remains—
The mantle's border in his hand,
His glazed eyes unremoved. The band
Of Jews—the pilgrims—all look on
Shocked or amazed.
But speech he won:
"No—yes: enchanted here!—her name?"
"Ruth, Nathan's daughter," said a Jew
Who kenned him now—the youth that came
Oft to the close; "but, thou—forbear;
The dawn's at hand and haste is due:

See, by her side, 'tis Agar there."
"Ruth? Agar?—art thou, God?—But ye—
All swims, and I but blackness see.—
How happed it? speak!"
          "The fever—grief:
'Twere hard to tell; was no relief."
"And ye—your tribe 'twas ye denied
Me access to this virgin's side
In bitter trial: take my curse!—
O blind, blind, barren universe!
Now am I like a bough torn down,
And I must wither, cloud or sun!—
Had I been near, this had not been.
Do spirits look down upon this scene?—
The message? some last word was left?"
          "For thee? no, none; the life was reft
Sudden from Ruth; and Agar died
Babbling of gulls and ocean wide—
Out of her mind."
          "And here's the furl
Of Nathan's faith: then perish faith—
'Tis perjured!—Take me, take me, Death!
Where Ruth is gone, me thither whirl,
Where'er it be!"
          "Ye do outgo
Mad Korah. Boy, this is the Dale

Of Doom, God's last assizes; so,
Curb thee; even if sharp grief assail,
Respect these precincts lest thou know
An ill."
          "Give way, quit thou our dead!"
Menaced another, striding out;
"Art thou of us? turn thee about!"
"Spurn—I'll endure; all spirit's fled
When one fears nothing.—Bear with me,
Yet bear!—Conviction is not gone
Though faith's gone: that which shall not be
It ought to be!"
          But here came on

With heavy footing, hollow heard,
Hebrews, which bare rude slabs, to place
Athwart the bodies when interred,
That earth should weigh not on the face;
For coffin was there none; and all
Was make-shift in this funeral.
Uncouthly here a Jew began

To re-adjust Ruth's cloak. Amain
Did Clarel push him; and, in hiss:
"Not thou—for me!—Alone, alone
In such bride-chamber to lie down!
Nay, leave one hand out—like to this—
That so the bridegroom may not miss
To kiss it first, when soon he comes.—
But 'tis not she!" and hid his face.

They laid them in the under-glooms—
Each pale one in her portioned place.
The gravel, from the bank raked down,
Dull sounded on those slabs of stone,
Grave answering grave—dull and more dull,
Each mass growing more, till either pit was full.

As up from Kedron dumb they drew,
Then first the shivering Clarel knew
Night's damp. The Martyr's port is won—
Stephen's; harsh grates the bolt withdrawn
And, over Olivet, comes on
Ash Wednesday in the gray of dawn.

Canto XXXI – Dirge

Stay, Death. Not mine the Christus-wand
Wherewith to charge thee and command:
I plead. Most gently hold the hand
Of her thou leadest far away;
Fear thou to let her naked feet
Tread ashes—but let mosses sweet
Her footing tempt, where'er ye stray.
Shun Orcus; win the moonlit land
Belulled—the silent meadows lone,
Where never any leaf is blown
From lily-stem in Azrael's hand.
There, till her love rejoin her lowly
(Pensive, a shade, but all her own)
On honey feed her, wild and holy;
Or trance her with thy choicest charm.
And if, ere yet the lover's free,
Some added dusk thy rule decree
That shadow only let it be
Thrown in the moon-Glade by the palm.

Day passed; and passed a second one,
A third—fourth—fifth; and bound he sate
In film of sorrow without moan—
Abandoned, in the stony strait
Of mutineer thrust on wild shore,
Hearing, beyond the roller's froth,
The last dip of the parting oar.
Alone, for all had left him so;
Though Rolfe, Vine, Derwent—each was loth,
How loth to leave him, or to go
Be first. From Vine he caught new sense
Developed through fate's pertinence.
Friendly they tarried—blameless went:
Life, avaricious, still demands
Her own, and more; the world is rent
With partings.
But, since all are gone,
Why lingers he, the stricken one?
Why linger where no hope can be?
Ask grief, love ask—fidelity
In dog that by the corse abides
Of shepherd fallen—abides, abides
Though autumn into winter glides,
Till on the mountain all is chill
And snow-bound, and the twain lie still.

How oft through Lent the feet were led
Of this chastised and fasting one
To neutral silence of the dead
In Kedron's gulf. One morn he sate
Down poring toward it from the gate
Sealed and named Golden. There a tomb,
Erected in time's recent day,
In block along the threshold lay
Impassable. From Omar's bloom
Came birds which lit, nor dreamed of harm,
On neighboring stones. His visage calm
Seemed not the one which late showed play
Of passion's throe; but here divine
No peace; ignition in the mine
Announced is by the rush, the roar:
These end; yet may the coal burn on—
Still slumberous burn beneath the floor
Of pastures where the sheep lie down.
Ere long a cheerful choral strain

He hears; 'tis an Armenian train
Embowered in palms they bear, which (green,
And shifting oft) reveal the mien
Of flamens tall and singers young
In festal robes: a rainbow throng,
Like dolphins off Madeira seen
Which quick the ship and shout dismay.
With the blest anthem, censers sway,
Whose opal vapor, spiral borne,
Blends with the heavens' own azure Morn
Of Palms; for 'twas Palm Sunday bright,
Though thereof he, oblivious quite,
Knew nothing, nor that here they came
In memory of the green acclaim
Triumphal, and hosanna-roll
Which hailed Him on the ass's foal
But unto Clarel that bright view
Into a dusk reminder grew:
He saw the tapers—saw again
The censers, singers, and the wreath
And litter of the bride of death
Pass through the Broken Fountain's lane;
In treble shrill and bass how deep
The men and boys he heard again
The undetermined contest keep
About the bier—the bier Armenian.
Yet dull, in torpor dim, he knew
That futile omen in review.

Yet three more days, and leadenly
From over Mary's port and arch,
On Holy Thursday, he the march
Of friars beheld, with litany
Filing beneath his feet, and bent
With crosses craped to sacrament
Down in the glenned Gethsemane.
Yes, Passion Week; the altars cower—
Each shrine a dead dismantled bower.

But when Good Friday dirged her gloom
Ere brake the morning, and each light
Round Calvary faded and the TOMB,
What exhalations met his sight:—
Illusion of grief's wakeful doom:
The dead walked. There, amid the train,
Wan Nehemiah he saw again—
With charnel beard; and Celio passed
As in a dampened mirror glassed;

Gleamed Mortmain, pallid as wolf-bone
Which bleaches where no man hath gone;
And Nathan in his murdered guise—
Sullen, and Hades in his eyes;
Poor Agar, with such wandering mien
As in her last blank hour was seen.
And each and all kept lonely state,
Yea, man and wife passed separate.
But Ruth—ah, how estranged in face!
He knew her by no earthly grace:
Nor might he reach to her in place.
And languid vapors from them go
Like thaw-fogs curled from dankish snow.

Where, where now He who helpeth us,
The Comforter?—Tell, Erebus!

Canto XXXIII - Easter

BUT ON THE THIRD DAY CHRIST AROSE;
And, in the town He knew, the rite
Commemorative eager goes
Before the hour. Upon the night
Between the week's last day and first,
No more the Stabat is dispersed
Or Tenebrae. And when the day,
The Easter, falls in calendar
The same to Latin and the array
Of all schismatics from afar—
Armenians, Greeks from many a shore—
Syrians, Copts—profusely pour
The hymns: 'tis like the choric gush
Of torrents Alpine when they rush
To swell the anthem of the spring.
That year was now. Throughout the fane,
Floor, and arcades in double ring
About the gala of THE TOMB,
Blazing with lights, behung with bloom—
What child-like thousands roll the strain,
The hallelujah after pain,
Which in all tongues of Christendom
Still through the ages has rehearsed
That Best, the outcome of the Worst.

Nor blame them who by lavish rite
Thus greet the pale victorious Son,

Since Nature times the same delight,
And rises with the Emerging One;
Her passion-week, her winter mood
She slips, with crape from off the Rood.
In soft rich shadow under dome,
With gems and robes repletely fine,
The priests like birds Brazilian shine:
And moving tapers charm the sight,
Enkindling the curled incense-fume:
A dancing ray, Auroral light.

Burn on the hours, and meet the day.
The morn invites; the suburbs call
The concourse to come forth—this way!
Out from the gate by Stephen's wall,
They issue, dot the hills, and stray
In bands, like sheep among the rocks;
And the Good Shepherd in the heaven,
To whom the charge of these is given,
The Christ, ah! counts He there His flocks?
But they, at each suburban shrine,
Grateful adore that Friend benign;
Though chapel now and cross divine
Too frequent show neglected; nay,
For charities of early rains
Rim them about with vernal stains,
Forerunners of maturer May,
When those red flowers, which so can please,
(Christ's-Blood-Drops named—anemones),
Spot Ephraim and the mountain-way.
But heart bereft is unrepaid
Though Thammuz' spring in Thammuz' glade
Invite; then how in Joel's glen?
What if dyed shawl and bodice gay
Make bright the black dell? what if they
In distance clear diminished be
To seeming cherries dropped on pall
Borne graveward under laden tree?
The cheer, so human, might not call
The maiden up; Christ is arisen:
But Ruth, may Ruth so burst the prison?

The rite supreme being ended now,
Their confluence here the nations part:
Homeward the tides of pilgrims flow,
By contrast making the walled town
Like a depopulated mart;
More like some kirk on week-day lone,

On whose void benches broodeth still
The brown light from November hill.

But though the freshet quite be gone—
Sluggish, life's wonted stream flows on.

Canto XXXIV - Via Crucis

Some leading thoroughfares of man
In wood-path, track, or trail began;
Though threading heart of proudest town,
They follow in controlling grade
A hint or dictate, nature's own,
By man, as by the brute, obeyed.

Within Jerusalem a lane,
Narrow, nor less an artery main
(Though little knoweth it of din),
In part suggests such origin.
The restoration or repair,
Successive through long ages there,
Of city upon city tumbled,
Might scarce divert that thoroughfare,
Whose hill abideth yet unhumbled
Above the valley-side it meets.
Pronounce its name, this natural street's:
The Via Crucis—even the way
Tradition claims to be the one
Trod on that Friday far away
By Him our pure exemplar shown.

'Tis Whitsun-tide. From paths without,
Through Stephen's gate by many a vein
Convergent brought within this lane,
Ere sun-down shut the loiterer out—
As 'twere a frieze, behold the train!
Bowed water-carriers; Jews with staves;
Infirm gray monks; over-loaded slaves;
Turk soldiers—young, with home-sick eyes;
A Bey, bereaved through luxuries;
Strangers and exiles; Moslem dames
Long-veiled in monumental white,
Dumb from the mounds which memory claims;
A half-starved vagrant Edomite;
Sore-footed Arab girls, which toil
Depressed under heap of garden-spoil;

The patient ass with panniered urn;
Sour camels humped by heaven and man,
Whose languid necks through habit turn
For ease for ease they hardly gain.
In varied forms of fate they wend—
Or man or animal, 'tis one:
Cross-bearers all, alike they tend
And follow, slowly follow on.

But, lagging after, who is he
Called early every hope to test,
And now, at close of rarer quest,
Finds so much more the heavier tree?
From slopes whence even Echo's gone,
Wending, he murmurs in low tone:
"They wire the world—far under sea
They talk; but never comes to me
A message from beneath the stone."

Dusked Olivet he leaves behind,
And, taking now a slender wynd,
Vanishes in the obscurer town.

Canto XXXV – Epilogue

If Luther's day expand to Darwin's year,
Shall that exclude the hope foreclose the fear?

Unmoved by all the claims our times avow,
The ancient Sphinx still keeps the porch of shade;
And comes Despair, whom not her calm may cow,
And coldly on that adamantine brow
Scrawls undeterred his bitter pasquinade.
But Faith (who from the scrawl indignant turns)
With blood warm oozing from her wounded trust,
Inscribes even on her shards of broken urns
The sign o' the cross—the spirit above the dust!

Yea, ape and angel, strife and old debate—
The harps of heaven and dreary gongs of hell;
Science the feud can only aggravate—
No umpire she betwixt the chimes and knell:
The running battle of the star and clod
Shall run forever—if there be no God.

Degrees we know, unknown in days before;

The light is greater, hence the shadow more;
And tantalized and apprehensive Man
Appealing—Wherefore ripen us to pain?
Seems there the spokesman of dumb Nature's train.
But through such strange illusions have they passed
Who in life's pilgrimage have baffled striven—
Even death may prove unreal at the last,
And stoics be astounded into heaven.

Then keep thy heart, though yet but ill-resigned—
Clarel, thy heart, the issues there but mind;
That like the crocus budding through the snow—
That like a swimmer rising from the deep—
That like a burning secret which doth go
Even from the bosom that would hoard and keep;
Emerge thou mayst from the last whelming sea,
And prove that death but routs life into victory.

END OF THE FOURTH AND FINAL PART

Herman Melville – A Short Biography

Herman Melville was born in New York City on August 1st, 1819, the third of eight children.

At the age of 7 Melville contracted scarlet fever which was to permanently diminish his eyesight. At this time Melville was described as being "very backwards in speech and somewhat slow in comprehension."

Melville attended the Albany Academy from October 1830 to October 1831, where he took the standard preparatory course; reading and spelling; penmanship; arithmetic; English grammar; geography; natural history; universal, Greek, Roman and English history; classical biography; and Jewish antiquities.

The reasons for Melville leaving the Academy after a year are unknown although his brothers continued their education there for a few more months.

In December, Melville's father returned from New York City by steamboat, but difficult weather forced him to travel the last 70 miles in an open carriage in freezing temperatures. A cold developed into delirium and by January 28th, not yet fifty, his father was dead. Melville, at home by now, most probably witnessed much of this event and two decades later he described scenes that must have been very similar in the death of Pierre's father in Pierre.

The family were now in very straitened times. Just 14 Melville took a job in a bank paying $150 a year that he obtained via his uncle, Peter Gansevoort, who was one of the directors of the New York State Bank.

Melville was briefly able to attend again the Albany Academy from October 1836 to March 1837, where he studied the classics.

After a failed stint as a surveyor he signed on to go to sea and travelled across the Atlantic to Liverpool and then on further voyages to the Pacific on adventures which would soon become the architecture of his novels. Whilst travelling he joined a mutiny, was jailed, fell in love with a South Pacific beauty and became known as a figure of opposition to the coercion of native Hawaiians to the Christian religion.

He drew from these experiences in his books Typee, Omoo, and White-Jacket. These were published as novels, the first initially in London in 1846.

They sold very well and enabled him to write full time although royalties were not vast. (During his career it is estimated his writing brought him no more than $10,000)

After a three-month courtship of Elizabeth Shaw, daughter of a prominent Boston family, her father was the Chief Justice of the Massachusetts Supreme Judicial Court, they decided to marry. Her father initially turned down Melville's request but on August 14th, 1847 they married. After initially settling in New York they moved to Massachusetts.

In September of 1850, Melville borrowed $3,000 from his father-in-law Lemuel Shaw to buy a 160-acre farm in Pittsfield. Melville christened the new home 'Arrowhead', due to the quantity of arrowheads dug up around the property during planting season.

That winter, Melville on an impulse paid a visit to the writer Nathaniel Hawthorne. At the time Hawthorne was finishing The House of the Seven Gables and "not in the mood for company". Hawthorne's wife Sophia entertained him while he waited for Hawthorne to come down for supper, and gave him copies of Twice-Told Tales and, The Grandfather's Chair. Melville, sensing a friendship developing, invited them to Arrowhead during the coming weeks. When Sophia agreed, he looked forward to "discussing the Universe with a bottle of brandy & cigars" with Hawthorne.

By 1851 his masterpiece, Moby Dick, was ready to be published. It is perhaps, and certainly at the time, one of the most ambitious novels ever written. However, it never sold out its initial print run of 3,000 and Melville's earnings on this masterpiece were a mere $556.37.

In succeeding years his reputation waned and he found life increasingly difficult. His family was growing, now four children, and a stable income was essential.

From 1853 to 1856, Melville began to publish his short stories in the growing magazine market, most notably "Bartleby, the Scrivener" (1853), "The Encantadas" (1854), and "Benito Cereno" (1855). These and others were later collected together and published in 1856 as the Piazza Tales.

In 1857, he travelled to England where, for the first time since 1852, he reunited with Hawthorne. He then went on to tour the Near East. The Confidence-Man was the last prose work that he published that same year. It received little attention.

With his finances in a disappointing state Melville took the advice of friends that a change in career was called for. For many others public lecturing had proved very rewarding. From late 1857 to 1860, Melville embarked upon three lecture tours, where he spoke mainly on Roman statuary and sightseeing in Rome. These lectures mocked the pseudo-intellectualism of lyceum culture. His words though were ignored by contemporary audiences.

In the 1860's he wrote many poems, many based on the Civil War. But there was no publisher for him and no audience.

In 1866, Melville's wife and her relatives used their influence to obtain a position for him as customs inspector for the City of New York, With his writings almost ignored they moved to New York where Melville joined the New York Customs house and worked there for the next 19 years.

For Melville his early promise and great talents seemed to be getting him nowhere in literary terms. Despite periods of drinking, depression and other ails Elizabeth stood by her husband despite calls from other family members and the marriage held together.

In 1876 he was at last able to publish privately his 16,000 line epic poem Clarel, in which a young American student of divinity travels to Jerusalem to renew his faith. It was to no avail. The book had an initial printing of 350 copies, but sales failed miserably, and the unsold copies were burned when Melville was unable to afford to buy them at cost.

On December 31st, 1885 Melville was at last able to retire. His wife had inherited several small legacies and with her astute ways it was enough to provide them with a reasonable income and Melville had enough to buy further precious books and supplies.

In these last few years Melville finished two poetry collections which were printed privately, although only 25 copies of each; John Marr and Other Sailors (1888) and Timoleon (1891).

Herman Melville, novelist, poet, short story writer and essayist, died at his home on September 28rh 1891 from cardiovascular disease.

He was interred in the Woodlawn Cemetery in The Bronx, New York City.

He was the first writer to have his works collected and published by the Library of America.

Herman Melville – A Concise Bibliography

Novels, Short Stories & Poetry

Typee: A Peep at Polynesian Life (1846)
Omoo: A Narrative of Adventures in the South Seas (1847)
Mardi: And a Voyage Thither (1849)
Redburn: His First Voyage (1849)
White-Jacket; or, The World in a Man-of-War (1850)
Moby-Dick; or, The Whale (1851)
Pierre: or, The Ambiguities (1852)
Isle of the Cross (1853 unpublished, and now lost)
Cock-A-doodle-Doo (Short story) (1852)

Bartleby, the Scrivener (Short story) (1853)

The Encantadas, or Enchanted Isles (Short story) (1854)

Poor Man's Pudding and Rich Man's Crumbs (Short story) (1854)

The Happy Failure (Short story) (1854)

The Lightning-Rod Man (Short story) (1854)

The Fiddler (Short story) (1854)

Benito Cereno (1855)

Israel Potter: His Fifty Years of Exile (1855)

The Paradise of Batchelors and the Tartarus of Maids (Short story) (1855)

The Bell-Tower (Short story) (1855)

Jimmy Rose (Short story) (1855)

The Gees (Short story) (1856)

I and My Chimney (Short story) (1856)

The Apple-Tree Story (Short story) (1856)

The Confidence-Man: His Masquerade (1857)

The Piazza (Short story) (1856)

Battle-Pieces and Aspects of the War (Poetry) (1866)

Clarel: A Poem and Pilgrimage in the Holy Land (Epic poem) (1876)

John Marr and Other Sailors (Poetry) (1888)

Timoleon (Poetry) (1891)

Billy Budd, Sailor (An Inside Narrative) (1891 unfinished, published posthumously in 1924)

Essays

Fragments from a Writing Desk, No. 1 (May 4, 1839)

Fragments from a Writing Desk, No. 2 (May 18, 1839)

Etchings of a Whaling Cruise (1847)

Authentic Anecdotes of 'Old Zack" (July 24 to September 11, 1847)

Mr Parkman's Tour (March 31, 1849)

Cooper's New Novel (April 28, 1849)

A Thought on Book-Binding (March 16, 1850)

Hawthorne and His Mosses (August 17 and August 24, 1850)

www.ingramcontent.com/pod-product-compliance
Lightning Source LLC
Chambersburg PA
CBHW060130050426
42448CB00010B/2057